MERSEYSIDE BLITZED

NEIL HOLMES

HALSGROVE

Dedication

This book is dedicated to my Grandparents.
To them and most of their generation,
these events were not just history,
but part of their life.

First published in Great Britain in 2012

British Library Cataloguing-in-Publication Data
A CIP record for this title is available from the British Library

ISBN 978 0 85704 129 6

Halsgrove
Halsgrove House,
Ryelands Business Park,
Bagley Road, Wellington, Somerset TA21 9PZ
Tel: 01823 653777   Fax: 01823 216796
email: sales@halsgrove.com

Part of the Halsgrove group of companies
Information on all Halsgrove titles is available at: www.halsgrove.com

Printed in China by Everbest Printing Co Ltd

Acknowledgements

THE MAJORITY OF the wartime photographs of the Birkenhead area are reproduced with kind permission of the Birkenhead Reference Library which holds the copyright for them. Most of the photographs of Bootle come from the Stewart Bale Archive, which helped in tracing the organisation that originally commissioned the images. This turned out in almost every case to be Bootle Corporation. The images are therefore reproduced with permission from Sefton Library Service which holds the copyright for them.

The wartime photograph of the Cammell Laird Shipyards on page 89 is reproduced with kind permission of the Wirral Archive Service, Wirral Council. Most of the Wallasey photographs are reproduced with kind permission of the Wallasey Reference Library which holds the copyright for them. I would like to thank the staff of all of these sources for the help and advice they provided. Once again I am indebted to Julia Hoffman for her help, advice and hard work compiling the index. My parents have also offered support and suggestions that proved invaluable.

I have attempted to locate the copyright owner for the historical images on the following pages without success, but would be pleased to hear from them so that proper acknowledgements can be made: 7, 10, 15, 16, 38, 40, 84, 120, and 128.

Author's Note

AS YOU WILL SEE this book primarily deals with the areas of Wallasey, Birkenhead, Bootle and Crosby, but this does not mean that these were the only areas of Merseyside where the bombs landed. Many bombs fell in Bebington for example, where more than 60 people were killed. Unfortunately it was not always easy to track down many good quality photographs for these other areas. Of those that did exist, many did not identify the building or road concerned, making a comparison impossible. The number of photographs in each chapter therefore represents the availability of wartime images as much as how badly bombed that area was.

Introduction

LIKE LIVERPOOL, the surrounding areas of Merseyside have their own dedicated books that relate the wartime experience of that particular borough. Whilst they are usually very informative and interesting, they unfortunately often lack any sense of connection to our modern day view of those towns. When entire streets have been swept away to build modern shopping centres it is difficult to relate to the scene of death and destruction that once took place there. Much of Merseyside has changed dramatically since the war, and each difference makes the wartime scenes seem that much more alien to our modern eyes.

Following the theme of *Liverpool Blitzed*, this book aims to address this problem by displaying a wartime image alongside a modern photograph showing as similar a viewpoint as possible. In doing so it allows the reader to visualise what it must have been like to stand in that spot more than seven decades ago, seeing the city change, often literally overnight. The areas covered by this book are some of the hardest hit in the whole country, with over 1300 people losing their lives and over 5000 houses demolished beyond repair.

The book will cover not just how the raids affected industries, docks and town halls but how they hurt the general public, showing the impact on houses, churches and cinemas. We should always remember though that each of these wartime photographs represents a story. At best this would be one of disruption and inconvenience, at worst one of serious injury or death, with lives tragically cut short. Recording all of these stories though would be nearly impossible, especially as many of those who experienced the events first hand have long since passed away.

That today's generation have not had to deal with rationing, incendiary bombs, evacuation, blackouts and air raid shelters is largely down to the courage, dedication and bravery of the ordinary men, women and children of the region. For the most part they went about their duty without official recognition or thanks, and many would not have sought any either. I sincerely hope that this book gives you a greater appreciation for those who lived through the events described.

Wallasey

LOCATED IN THE Northeastern corner of the Wirral, Wallasey was originally almost an island, largely cut off from the remainder of the peninsula by the Wallasey Pool and marshy areas around Bidston Moss and Leasowe. It was this isolated nature that gave the town its name. Invading Anglo-Saxon tribes drove the native population to this "island" and called it Wealasey. This derived from their words for stranger, Wealas (Wales comes from the same root) and the suffix "ey" which meant island, or dry place.

Although it has a long history, the area was for the most part sparsely populated until the nineteenth century. In the early 1800s it became a popular place to retire for merchants and sea captains who often built large houses overlooking the Mersey. In 1830 a merchant called James Atherton purchased land in the area and began to develop it into a resort, calling it New Brighton after the south coast Regency town. By the middle of the century a series of docks, collectively known as the Great Float were constructed around the area of Wallasey Pool and many industries grew up around these.

The coming of steam ferries at Seacombe, Egremont and New Brighton, followed by the Mersey Railway in 1866 opened the area up even further, making commuting to Liverpool cheap and fast. This ushered in a major increase in the pace of housing development, especially in the Liscard and Wallasey Village areas. By the war this had spread even further afield to areas such as Leasowe and Moreton and the population of the borough was in the region of 90,000.

Throughout the second half of the nineteenth century there was an increase in local government power that culminated in the application for incorporation as a Municipal Borough. This was finally accepted in 1910. The borough's coat of arms (right) incorporate the Wirral Horn, three wheat sheafs to represent Cheshire and an old sailing ship representing the town's maritime history. The motto "Audemus dum cavemus" means

"We are bold whilst we are cautious". Three years later County Borough status was granted.

Wallasey played an important role in the region's war effort. Although known as Birkenhead Docks, the boundary between Birkenhead and Wallasey ran roughly down the centre of the Great Float, so many of the facilities were in fact in Wallasey. These docks dealt with their own fair share of goods and convoys and by the outbreak of World War Two they handled around 13% of the trade coming into the Port of Liverpool. They were also used for ship repair and conversion work and throughout the war various smaller escort vessels such as destroyers, frigates and corvettes called the docks their home.

The borough also helped the war effort in other ways, for example New Brighton at this time was still a popular resort. Although it's Tower (which

AUDEMUS·DUM·CAVEMUS

was taller than Blackpool's) had been demolished twenty years earlier, the ballroom it once rested on remained and proved extremely popular with military personnel stationed in the area. The nearby New Palace and the Tower Stadium were also taken over by the American Army and used for the storage of goods and maintenance of vehicles. A short distance away the resort also boasted a large open air swimming pool with room for 4000 bathers! Alongside these attractions the town posessed many good cinemas, theatres and dance halls.

The borough also defended itself through a variety of means. Several anti-aircraft batteries were placed in Wallasey, including an unusual type sited in the Warren Golf Course. The 104th Rocket Anti-Aircraft Battery used projectors which fired 20 rockets at a time, in a volley that would have proven deadly to any low-flying enemy plane.

Formed in early 1942 the battery comprised of no fewer than 64 projectors (two of which are seen below) which were manned on a rota by the Home Guard. By the time the battery became operational however the raids on Merseyside were thankfully over, and the projectors never fired a rocket in anger. The borough also deployed a large number of barrage balloons to force enemy planes to bomb from a greater height, thus reducing their accuracy.

During the war 320 people were killed, 275 were seriously injured and 628 lightly injured in the borough. Some 1150 houses were completely demolished and a little over 17,000 were damaged. The 509 alerts and 43 separate raids on the borough ensured that the civil defence workers were kept active.

The *Royal Daffodil II* was a Wallasey ferry-boat that entered service in 1934. During the war she saw service ferrying troops to and from liners anchored in the river. On the night of 7/8 May 1941 she was struck by a bomb which landed near the engine room. One member of the engine room crew present that night was blown clear of the boat, but he survived the experience, losing his false teeth rather than his life! The boat sank where it had been moored for the night, at Secombe Ferry landing stage. In July 1942 she was raised, cleaned up and put back into service, a measure of how important she was to both the Corporation and the Port of Liverpool. Before the war *Royal Daffodil II* had been one of the most luxurious ferry-boats in the Wallasey Corporation's fleet. Fourteen months at the bottom of the Mersey however left it filled with mud and silt, damaging much of the plush interior, which was not replaced for several years.

First recorded in 1515, Seacombe Ferry remains in use today, although the landing stage has undergone yet another facelift since the war. The tall tower just to the left of centre is a ventilation shaft for the Kinsgway Tunnel which connects Wallasey with Liverpool. Just to the right of this can be seen the smaller tower of Wallasey Town Hall. This photograph was taken from the modern day *Royal Daffodil*, a 1960s' vessel that was originally part of the Birkenhead Corporation's fleet. Alongside the *Snowdrop* and *Royal Iris* it operates a daily service.

This photograph shows the damage done to numbers 9 and 11 Palatine Road in Seacombe. It was taken after the raid on 10 August 1940. Although both buildings seem relatively intact, they have lost their windows and doors. The owners have improvised house numbers with chalk on the walls. As this was the first raid on Wallasey sights such as this were still unique in the borough and probably attracted attention from passers-by and children, many of whom would soon experience this kind of event first hand. Palatine Road also had a network of brick street shelters, two of which can be seen in the photograph below. The white paint marks were placed on the edges of shelters to warn drivers during the blackout.

After the raid the minor damage was repaired and both houses are still standing today.

The Central Hydraulic Tower in Tower Road provided power for the operation of dock gates and bridges throughout the dock estate. It was not possible to determine with any certainty when the damage was inflicted, but it's quite probable that it was during a raid on the night of 17/18 September 1940 as the nearby East Float and Morpeth Docks were both hit then.

As can be seen from the different coloured bricks, the building was repaired after the war, albeit in a simpler style and without part of the tower. No longer used for its original purpose, the building is in a sorry state.

Winston Churchill came to Wirral on 25 April 1941, to see for himself the damage caused by the raids of the previous month. In this photograph he can be seen on the Dock Road with the Swan Hotel in the background. The Prime Minister toured Birkenhead and Wallasey, viewing damage in places like Malaby Street (see page 58) and Brattan Road (page 81), before inspecting the Cammell Laird shipyards (page 89). The car belonged to the then Mayor of Birkenhead, Alderman Short.

Although no longer open the Swan is still standing making a comparison easy. Almost directly opposite this once stood *U534*, a recovered German submarine that is now located at Woodside Ferry Terminal.

Buchanan's Flour Mills once occupied a large site on either side of the Dock Road in Seacombe. Their site was one of many spread across the docks in this area which formed what was then the largest grain milling centre in the whole of Europe. The company were the first to open a mill in the docks, doing so in 1894. The damage seen here took place in March 1941. On the left a large metal walkway which connected the company's premises on each side has fallen onto the road. The presence of handcarts, workmen and a truck suggest that the photograph was probably taken shortly after the raid, perhaps later the next day. Although a considerable amount of work would be needed to clear the heavy metal walkway from the cobbled surface, the Dock Road was a major transport artery and would have been considered a high priority for repairs and clearance. Buchanan's were able to restore some production capability by May of that year, quicker than might be expected given the damage seen here.

Buchanan's Mills remained on the site until the early 1960s when their mills, like so many around them closed. They were eventually demolished in the late 1970s. Today the site is empty and used, if at all for storage. In the distance on the right can be seen the only two remaining mills on the Dock Road. Although they were used by various companies for their intended purpose until 1999 they have since been converted into luxury flats. In the distance one of the skyscrapers over in Liverpool can just be made out.

This photograph appeared in the *Daily Post* on 23 December 1940 and shows number 32 Brougham Road in Seacombe. Clearly the house suffered a near miss which cratered the road and threw a nearby motor car over the front wall and up against the house. Fortunately most of the damage seems slight, although it will no doubt be a little while before the car can be removed and the road repaired. No-one seems to have been killed in the road that night and the biggest problem will probably be the damaged mains pipe that is causing the flooding in the foreground.

Number 32 seems to have suffered no ill effect from the wartime damage and is still standing today.

On the night of 31 August/1 September 1940 bombs landed in Brighton Street, damaging buildings and cratering the road. This was only the third raid on Wallasey, but the work of the wardens in the area had already brought praise from local controllers and further afield. Although they had barely had a taste of what was in store for the region in the coming year or so, the fact that there were relatively few casualties in an area of dense terraced housing was at least in part down to the warden's hard work, even if it did owe something on occasion to luck.

The large building second from the right is the Brighton Hotel, which is on the corner of Brighton Street and Buchanan Road. The premises on the left were occupied by (left to right) a grocers, tobacconists and chemists. Just across the road from here is Wallasey Town Hall, which received its own hammering on the same night. In this area one person was killed and another three were injured that night. A hasty barricade has been erected and men are already at work repairing the damage. The surrounding roads were also damaged as Wallasey bore the brunt of that night's raids.

Since the war two of the three premises on the left have been demolished and replaced by a car park, but the Brighton Hotel remains and is still open for business today.

Littledale Road runs between Brighton Street and Liscard Road. In this photograph taken on 6 November 1940 the King (in military uniform just to the right of centre) and Queen (slightly behind and to the left of the king) are visiting the borough to see the damage for themselves. We can only guess whether they saw the large number of young boys cheering and playing around on the top of the street

shelters! On the same day they also visited Bedford Road (see page 25) and the Town Hall. In today's security conscious world it seems remarkable that the head of state would be allowed to walk through streets with the public so close by. The Royal Family remained popular throughout the war though, especially after Buckingham Palace was bombed during the blitz on London. The thought that anyone would try to hurt either of them would have been alien to almost everyone in the crowd, but no doubt one or two bodyguards in plain clothes are present just in case. The damage that can be seen in the background was caused on the night of Wallasey's third raid, which occurred on August 30/31 1940. Numbers 24 and 26 were hit and two women injured, but fortunately both of them survived. Littledale Road was named after Harold Littledale who owned nearby Liscard Hall until his death in 1899.

Even though only one of the buildings in the wartime photograph seems to have been demolished outright, numbers 22-28 Littledale Road were eventually demolished. They have been replaced by garages that local people can rent.

This image showing damage to Wallasey Town Hall appeared in the *Liverpool Echo* on 2 September 1940 under the title of "Damaged North-Western Town Hall". This was at a time when newspapers still adhered to the principal of not giving specific town or city names in an attempt to deny intelligence to the enemy. It was probably taken around the same time as the one on page 13. One bomb penetrated the roof of the south-western corner of building and badly damaged its organ and concert room. The foundation stone of the building was laid by George V in 1914 but during World War One the building was used as a military hospital that treated more than 3000 patients. It was returned to the borough in 1919 and opened officially as a Town Hall a year later. Despite being located on a prominent site in King Street this is in fact the rear of the building since it was built to face the river with steps on the far side of the building leading down to the promenade. This led to it being given the nickname of a "back-to-front" Town Hall.

Since the creation of Wirral Borough Council in 1974 the Council meetings are held in this building, although many of the council offices are now housed in post-war buildings on either side of the Town Hall. The modern photograph was taken from a slightly different angle as the trees on the left blocked a direct comparison.

The first ferry at Egremont was built in 1828 by Captain J. Askew, an investor in land. He also purchased land in the surrounding area on which he built his house, named Egremont after his birthplace in Cumberland. Eventually the area came to be known by the same name. The ferry was bought by the Wallasey Local Board in 1860 and operated services to and from the Pier Head in Liverpool. In 1932 the pier was rammed by a tanker and so badly damaged that it was out of use for a year. On 13 May 1941 the coaster ship *Newlands* lost control in the river and rammed the pier, once again putting it out of action. The searchlight post that was based on the floating stage was recovered and placed on the remains of the pier instead. The tall chimneys across the river are part of the Clarence Dock Power Station. To the left of this are the Stanley Dock Tobacco Warehouse and the Victoria Tower.

The ferry was never repaired and was eventually dismantled in 1946. It has since been replaced by a breakwater. The Clarence Dock Power Station was demolished in the mid 1990s. In the distance on the right are the skyscrapers of Liverpool City Centre. The ferry buildings that stood just behind where this photograph was taken were also demolished, their place now taken by a car park. This contains a speaker's corner, a place where open air debate, speaking and discussion are permitted.

Perhaps one of the more unusual resources that the region was able to deploy in dealing with the air raids was the Fireboat Section. Affectionately known as "The Water Rats" the section initially consisted of four boats, each of which carried four fire fighting pumps. They were used extensively during the air raids, with crews doing a 48 hour shift on board, before returning to shore for 24 hours rest. Each crew consisted of seven men, some of whom had little or no experience of life at sea, although this was no barrier as the craft mostly operated in the docks and on the river. One of the four was caught up in the explosion of the *Malakand* in Huskisson dock and had to be taken out of commission, but the boats soon proved worth their weight in gold and the section was expanded until it eventually numbered 20 vessels, crewed by 150 personnel. In this posed photograph the crew are demonstrating the different pumps, some of which could throw a jet of water 150 feet. In the background the tower of Wallasey Town Hall can be seen, along with the steps leading up to it from the promenade.

The modern view was taken from one of the Mersey Ferries. The Town Hall still survives, although it is no longer the only prominent building on the skyline. Just to its left can be seen one of Wallasey's blocks of high rise of flats, whereas just to the right of centre the tower of St Mary's church in Liscard can be made out.

This photograph shows numbers 1-7 Chatsworth Avenue which is off Liscard Road, roughly opposite where Liscard Hall once stood. Despite the rather extensive damage to the buildings no-one was killed here in the December raids that caused this destruction. The raids struck especially hard at this kind of area due to its relative proximity of the Mersey shoreline. The bombers would often try to target shipping in the river where possible. Nearby Liscard Hall was fortunate and survived the raids intact. Although this was originally built as Moors Hey House as the home of Sir John Tobin in 1832, by the time of the war it was used as an art school and its former grounds had become Central Park. The park's lake was often used as an emergency water supply to fight fires started by the air raids, with water pumped directly from it.

The damaged buildings were repaired after the war leaving no indication of the destruction the raids inflicted. Liscard Hall remained in use as an art college until the 1980s when it was leased to an organisation involved in Youth Training Schemes.

The author attended this college for around a year. Sadly this organisation folded in 2003 and the building remained empty for the several years. In 2008 vandals managed to set fire to part of the building. This caused so much damage that it unfortunately had to be demolished shortly after.

Just off Liscard Road near its junction with Mill Lane is Croxteth Avenue. This wartime view shows numbers 2-10. Despite the dreadful damage that can be seen here no-one was killed in any of these buildings, which were hit during December 1940. In the upper right of the photograph a gentleman can be seen gingerly making his way back to the street over the rubble. Given the bundle he is carrying under his arm, the presence of other people and the handcart on the right it is quite likely that he lived at that property, or perhaps was helping the family that did. Sadly the war brought out the worst in some, and people had to recover any belongings as quickly as possible to avoid any possibility of looting. Research has suggested that as many as

10,000 cases of this were reported nationwide. This was a tricky problem for the authorities to deal with, as in some cases the guilty included individuals in positions of authority. Officially the crime of looting could carry the death penalty, but this could easily have exaggerated the rumours of martial law that were already rife in places like Liverpool. Punishments therefore varied, but in London sentences were handed down of up to eight years hard labour.

Most of the road was rebuilt after the war, with this particular section now occupied with business premises and modern housing.

This photograph shows the remains of 48-52 Leominster Road, Liscard which were destroyed in a raid on 21/22 December 1940. The only fatality in this location seems to have been the 61-year-old Clara Birchall who lived at number 50. The tall chimney in the background is probably part of the Mill Lane Hospital. This was originally built as an isolation hospital dealing with infectious diseases such as diphtheria and scarlet fever. During the war an additional section was added for soldiers stationed nearby that were in need of isolation. On the night of 6 May 1941 part of the hospital was hit by a high explosive bomb that killed two children. A parachute mine was also stuck in a nearby tree, forcing an evacuation of the hospital. This was done with assistance from the priest of nearby St Alban's church and several off-duty hospital staff members. Between them they led patients through the gap in Leominster Road that can be seen here and on to safety. The evacuated patients were initially housed in the nearby Egerton Grove School, but were later moved to Clatterbridge Hospital for the duration of the repairs, which took three months.

After the war the houses were rebuilt in much the same style as those found elsewhere in the road. Mill Lane Hospital remains open to this day although it is now known as Victoria Central Hospital.

This view shows a parade which took place on Victory in Empire Day on 19 May 1945. The band in the front is about to pass into Wallasey Road, whilst the remainder of the procession are in Liscard Road. This photograph was probably taken from the upper floor of the Capitol, one of Wallasey's most popular cinemas. Burton were one of the country's favourite men's clothing stores, but even with the war in Europe won, rationing would remain in place on clothes for another four years. Firms like Burton turned their efforts towards war work such as making uniforms for the armed forces. The tall building on the left hand side of the photo is probably the former St Mary's School, by this date occupied by business premises.

Almost all of the buildings that are in the original photograph have long since gone. This part of Liscard Road has now been renamed Liscard Way. Although Burton still occupy part of the old site, it is now mainly a bank. Behind this, out of sight is the Cherry Tree Shopping Centre. The roundabout in the foreground of the wartime photograph has been replaced with a traffic island and traffic lights. The Capitol Cinema closed in 1974, later to reopen for a period as a bingo hall.

Lancaster Avenue originally ran from Withen's Lane to Wimbledon Street. In the early morning of 12 March 1941 several communal shelters and houses nearby were struck by a series high explosive bombs, resulting in thirty deaths. Although the archive records have four photographs labelled Lancaster Avenue, only this one actually shows it. The other three show Wimbledon Street from the junction of the two. Wimbledon Street was considered important enough to be cleared of debris by the time of the photographs. Most of the houses on one side of the street had been badly damaged, so the rubble was simply pushed to one side, allowing traffic to pass along it. Lancaster Avenue remained blocked by the rubble seen here. The men in the foreground must have felt that any effort was in vain, however this area was also the scene of a remarkable escape. Three and a half days after the raid workers were clearing away rubble nearby when they heard the cries of a child. Working with great care they managed to clear a safe route to the noise and found a tiny baby girl, somehow sheltered by the bodies of her parents. She was rescued and taken to Victoria Central Hospital, where she made an amazing recovery.

The construction of the modern Manor Road Police station shortened Lancaster Avenue slightly, so it no longer connects to Wimbledon Street. This comparison was therefore taken slightly further up the Avenue, which shows very little sign of the wartime events that occurred nearby. In the background on the left the tower of St Mary's church can be seen in both photographs.

During the raid on 21/22 December 1940 several bombs landed in the area of Withen's Lane, with one landing near its junction with Urmson Road. The demolished house shown here was number 61 Withen's Lane and three ladies were killed there. Annie Chatham aged 79 and Ethel Papin aged 55 were killed outright. Ethel was a member of the local ARP control service, a section that would co-ordinate the rescue service's response to the raids. Ellen Chatham aged 57 was taken to the Cottage Hospital in Claremount Road, but sadly died the next day of her injuries. Number 63 Withen's Lane was badly damaged but no-one seems to have been hurt there. Just across Withen's Lane from here was Wallasey Grammar School and a short distance behind the camera is St Mary's church. This area also suffered damage on the night of 14 October 1940 when bombs hit numbers 42, 44, 87 and 89 Withen's Lane, causing injury to one male and two females but no fatalities. The white

markings on the corner are to help drivers during the blackout.

Both 61 and 63 were later demolished to be replaced by the small block of flats seen here. Both the nearby church and school are still standing.

This photograph shows 117 and 119 Rake Lane, both of which seem to have been badly damaged, but fortunately no fatalities accompanied such widespread destruction. To the left of this photograph is Rake Lane Cemetery. Amongst those buried here is Captain William Turner who commanded the *Lusitania* on its fateful final voyage in 1915. A victim of the First World War, it was torpedoed and sunk off the coast of Ireland with the loss of 1198 people. Despite attempts by the admiralty to pin the blame on him, Captain Turner was exonerated at the board of enquiry. Another captain laid to rest here is Stanley Lord who was in charge of the SS *Californian* on 15 April 1912. On that fateful night his ship was much closer to the *Titanic* when the famous ship sank than most others, but a series of errors and unlucky coincidences meant that his ship did not come to the floundering giant's aid. Despite fierce criticism, Captain Lord would defend the decisions he took that night right up until his death in 1962.

Both houses were rebuilt after the war but only one bears any resemblance to the original style.

The demolished buildings in the centre of this view were numbers 1, 3 and 5 Bedford Road. On the left can be seen the rear of houses in Earlston Road. The damage seen here was done on 14 October 1940 and two people were injured. The King and Queen visited Wallasey on 6 November 1940 and met with a group of bombed out women here. The road is very short as out of shot to the right of here is Rake Lane Cemetery, which contains a memorial to the people of Wallasey who were killed in the blitz and as was mentioned on the previous page several graves of famous people. Flight Sergeant Ray Holmes was a Hurricane fighter pilot who spotted a Dornier bomber that was apparently trying to bomb Buckingham Palace in London. On attacking it he found that his guns had jammed, so rammed the plane instead, slicing off its tail and bringing both planes crashing to the ground. He bailed out, survived the war and after a long life was laid to rest in 2005. A short distance down Earlston Road to the left is Wallasey Central Library. Originally this was a private house, at one point owned by John Marsden (see the next page) but it was bought by the corporation in 1898 and turned into a public library and reading rooms. An extension was later added in 1911, but a wing was demolished by a bomb during the war.

Since the war all three destroyed houses have been rebuilt in almost exactly the same style as before and the houses in Earlston Road have been repaired.

This is the section of Rake Lane known as Stroude's corner. It is named after the drapery firm owned by Benjamin Stroude, which stood on the far left, at the corner with Magazine Lane. The premises shown here, which included a hairdressers, butchers, greengrocers and stationers, were all damaged on the night of 10 August 1940, during the first raid on the borough. The raid inflicted thirty two casualties and caused considerable property damage. These buildings appear to have escaped with relatively light damage and no-one seems to have been killed here that night. Rake Lane was also hit in December 1940 and May 1941. Just behind and to the left of where this photograph was taken stood the old Liscard Congregational Church. This was paid for by John Marsden who owned Liscard Castle, a nineteenth-century turreted house that gave its name to Castle and Turret Roads. The church opened in 1844 and was damaged in the war. Afterwards it was repaired and re-opened in 1954, only to be demolished in 1978.

Most of the buildings have survived until today intact, apart from one of them on the far left which seems to have been demolished. A single builder's and plumbing merchants occupies the premises in the foreground. This area is an especially familiar one for the author as his paternal grandparents lived in nearby Sandheys Road when he was growing up.

This photograph shows the junction of Seabank Road in the foreground and Magazine Lane on the left. Since the photograph appears in the local archives without a date it is difficult to determine what incident this represents, as both roads were hit more than once during the war.

Fortunately the damage here was relatively light and both the cratered road and damaged houses in the background have long since been repaired.

Dalmorton Road is just off Seabank Road. The houses shown in this photograph are numbers 69-75. Four people were killed here during the raid on 20 December 1940. Marjorie Cain lived at number 69 and the Finn family (Ernest, Winifred and their 11 month old son George) lived at number 71. In the background on the right can be seen a barrage balloon over the Mersey, which is only a short distance from here. Towards the far end of Seabank Road many of the roads run straight downhill to the promenade. It is speculated that this may have confused the Germans as they may have resembled a series of slipways for launching ships, similar to those seen at Cammell Laird shipyards. The government also made deliberate attempts to confuse the enemy, setting up the National Decoy Authority. Its aim was to construct a network of dummy sites around major urban areas. These would consist of formations of lights designed to mimic a city with an inefficient blackout in place, pyrotechnics to resemble impacting incendiaries and larger fires that looked like major blazes in docklands or city centres. The enemy raiders had very limited bomb aiming equipment and would

generally target such concentrations if a specific area could not be identified. Placed in rural areas the plan was to make the enemy's night bombers drop their payload into fields and hills. Although not always successful any wasted bombs were welcome.

All of the houses have been rebuilt since the war in largely the same style.

This photograph shows a part of Grosvenor Road in New Brighton which was cratered during the raid on 1 November 1940. During this attack there was a particularly heavy thunderstorm which damaged a number of barrage balloons. These large balloons were used extensively on Merseyside in an attempt to hinder low flying German bombers. The lightly damaged building behind the crater is number 19 Grosvenor Road, occupied by a riding school, garage and social club. Just to the rear of this building was New Brighton Tower. Once the tallest structure in the country, the tower itself was removed between 1919 and 1921, leaving the main building below. This housed one of the largest ballrooms in the United Kingdom and a theatre.

This remained a popular destination during the war, whilst the basement was used as a communal shelter. The surrounding grounds included a fairground, New Brighton Football Club's ground and a boating lake that included gondolas.

Number 19 was later used as a laundry, but was eventually demolished and replaced with sheltered housing. The Tower Ballroom remained a popular destination for many years after the war, with acts like Little Richard, the Rolling Stones and even The Beatles appearing there. Sadly in 1969 the building suffered a major fire and was demolished shortly after. The grounds have since been redeveloped.

1223 people who were killed or injured in the borough during the war were victims of those three nights. With Britain and the Commonwealth standing virtually alone in the fight against Hitler and the threat of invasion seemingly only postponed, this normally festive period must have seemed especially bleak and local people would have had little to celebrate. Even during this harsh time however the British public were able to dig deep and continue to support the war effort. Everyone seemed to do their best to contribute. Some people raised £50 through collecting small change whilst Rotary Clubs raised £10,000 from the collection of old gold and silver. Events were frequently held to promote the purchasing of National War Bonds or National Savings Accounts and included the students of Liverpool University staging a mock hanging of Adolf Hitler!

The large building in the foreground stood at the junction of Pickering Road and Rowson Street. At the outbreak of the war it was the premises of a motor engineer company called Fraser Apperley and Sons. The damage seen here, like so much inflicted on Wallasey occurred during the three night period from 20 to 23 December 1940. Nearly a third of the

The premises of Fraser Apperley and sons were later demolished, but the link to the past is retained since they have been replaced by the premises of a motor group, which also has a garage on the right in Pickering Road.

The Roman Catholic church of Saint Peter and Saint Paul once stood at the junction of Hope Street and Rowson Street in New Brighton. The church was consecrated in 1881 and a school connected to the church also stood on Hope Street. Just out of shot on the right stood one of the town's police stations.

The church was demolished shortly after and has since been replaced by a supermarket car park. The church had in fact already been surpassed by the construction in 1935 of St Peter and Paul church, which still stands today in Atherton Street. Due to its large dome and prominent site on a hill close to the river, the second church (left) became a familiar sight, especially to sailors approaching the River Mersey who nicknamed it "The Dome of Home". The former police station is now occupied by council offices.

These photographs show number 2 (top right) and 4 Sandringham Drive. Both suffered extensive damage during the night of 9 January 1941 and these photographs were presumably taken only a short time later due to the rubble still being in situ. It's quite possible that the lady walking across the rubble in the front of number 2 lived there. White curtains hanging out of the windows, such as those at number 4 gave rise to an often repeated rumour that local people were offering a white flag of surrender. Anyone familiar with the people of this area however knew better, it would take more than being bombed out to destroy their spirit.

Since the war the houses at this end of Sandringham Drive were rebuilt in a more modern style.

This photograph shows numbers 16-20 Warren Drive which were hit sometime during the raids between 12 and 14 March 1941, although this photograph was taken around a week later. Fortunately there were no fatalities, despite the heavy damage each has clearly suffered. The people who lived here were lucky as this was Wallasey's second period of sustained raids. A particularly troublesome aspect of those three nights was the deployment of parachute mines. Between these and the more common high explosive and incendiary bombs, March 1941 became the worst month Wallasey suffered in the entire war. During these three days alone 186 people were killed, 196 people seriously injured, 251 slightly injured and 10,000 people were made homeless in the borough. Fortunately this was followed by several weeks when the area suffered no raids at all, allowing it much needed time to recover. Between 1902 and 1933 electric trams ran down Warren Drive on one of the three routes that operated between Seacombe and New Brighton. By the war though the tram system had been dismantled, with buses and trains taking up the slack The electric tram's time in service had been so short that the man who drove the first one was able to return and drive the last!

Although all of these buildings were repaired or rebuilt after the war, the growth of hedges and trees prevents a better comparison.

Sandymount Drive runs between Mount Road and Rockland Road and the house in this view is number 9. It is not known at what date this damage was done, but no-one was killed in the building and it is not singled out in the police reports for special mention. This is not particularly surprising as during busy periods such as between 12 and 14 March 1941, there were so many incidents that there simply was not time to record them all. At the top of Sandymount Drive on the far side of Mount Road is the Wallasey Corporation Reservoir, which was built in 1886. This is an underground store of water so large that a boat was kept there for getting around it. The water tower next door to the reservoir was built in 1905 and is a Grade II listed building, as well as being a prominent local landmark.

After the war the house was rebuilt, leaving no reminder for today's owners of the sight that would have greeted the wartime occupiers when they emerged from the safety of their shelter.

This photograph shows the damage suffered by 29 and 31 Beverley Road on the night of 1 November 1941. Two people were killed in Wallasey that night, but neither lived in this street. Although this was the last raid on the borough, it was nonetheless a trying one as many of the bombs were of a high calibre. It would be small consolation to the owners that their houses would be amongst the last victims in the area of the Luftwaffe's raids.

Seeing the remarkable level of destruction inflicted on the two houses, it comes as something of a surprise to find modern houses of almost the same style standing in their place. This tendency to rebuild rather than going back to the drawing board is more often the case in the suburbs, where the pre-war housing was of a superior quality. In the town centres, especially in Bootle where so many pre-war houses were lost, the bombings created an opportunity to build better housing that would replace the often cramped terraces. Unfortunately this was not always successful, such as when tower blocks were constructed in the 1950s and 1960s. The immediate post-war period saw great housing shortages that the authorities found difficult to resolve. One idea was to construct prefabricated houses (known as prefabs). Quick and cheap to produce, over 150,000 were eventually used throughout the country. Although only designed to last ten years some are still standing today, a testament to the quality of their construction.

The Willows is a short road just off Grove Road. This photograph was taken on 10 April 1941, but it is not known on what date the raid took place. A bomb has clearly struck number 12 on the left, demolishing most of it and damaging number 10. It is quite possible that the damage was done during the raid on 8 April, but this concentrated primarily on the Liscard and Moreton areas, although a stray bomb is not out of the question. This raid proved especially difficult as many delayed action bombs were used. This required the civil defence authorities to evacuate the area in order to limit any casualties in the event that the bomb disposal squads were unable to defuse the device. Another possibility is that the house was one more victim of the raids between 12 and 14 March 1941 which wreaked so much havoc on the borough. This seems less likely however as the ruins would normally have been made safer in the intervening month. The photograph also contains the rather unusual sight of a bed hanging precariously in what was presumably the front bedroom of number 12. It seems unlikely that anyone was sleeping in this room during the raid since no-one was killed in the road by enemy action, and it's hard to imagine anyone surviving such damage.

Since the war the house has been rebuilt in exactly the same style.

line had been electrified shortly before the war. On the same night the railway embankment by Wallasey Village Station was also struck by bombs. This was the first time that the civil defences of this part of Wallasey had been tested. The borough, like most authorities divided itself into groups, with each being responsible for a specific area. Both stations came under Group 9, which covered most of the Wallasey Village area. Prior to this date the raids had mostly concentrated on those parts of the borough that were closer to the Mersey. Sadly this would not be the last night this group's area was attacked.

This is the rear of Windsors Garage which stands in Wallasey Village, opposite its junction with Grove Road. The building was damaged during the raid on 21 December 1940. Just a short distance behind where this photograph was taken stands Wallasey Grove Road Station, but at this time it was still known just as Wallasey Station. Opened in 1888 the

It is unlikely that many of those who use Wallasey Grove Road Station every day are aware of the scene of destruction that would have greeted them upon leaving the station that cold wintry morning. Windsors, a company founded in 1921, still occupy the building, which was repaired after the war.

This photograph was taken in Wallasey Village, looking towards its junction with Leasowe Road in the distance. In the middle of the photograph people are working to clear some of the debris of a raid in March 1941. This section of Wallasey Village contained the usual collection of local shops including a branch of the Co-Operative on the corner of Lycett Road. The building at the far left was a dairy and stores owned by a Mrs Amy Scragham. A short distance behind the camera is the famous Cheshire Cheese public house which was slightly damaged during the war. Rumour has it that King William III visited an earlier incarnation of the pub on his way to Ireland. Beyond the junction with Leasowe Road stood of the Coliseum Cinema (formerly the Cosmo Theatre) which was also hit during the raids. It was not as fortunate as the Cheshire Cheese however and was demolished shortly afterwards.

Although several of the buildings in the wartime photograph remain, they have changed ownership many times over the intervening years. A branch of the Co-Operative is a survivor, but has now moved to the site on the far left of the photograph, into the gap that the Luftwaffe created.

Birkenhead

LIKE ITS NEIGHBOUR to the north, Birkenhead was little more than a hamlet until the beginning of the nineteenth century, but it has been a place of importance for much longer. The town's name is thought to derive either from the nearby River Birket, or from the birch trees that once grew around the Woodside area. In Birkenhead Priory it contains the oldest standing building on Merseyside. Founded in 1150 by Hamo de Massey, the priory was operated by Benedictine Monks who used a rowing boat to cross the Mersey. In 1330 King Edward II granted the priors and their successors the rights to operate a ferry there forever.

Birkenhead remained of relatively low importance however until the rise of Liverpool as a major port. This brought an improvement in the ferry services between the two, which in turn lead to merchants buying up land to build their homes amid the pleasant surroundings found on the Wirral. The arrival from Liverpool of one of these, a Scotsman named William Laird changed the town forever. He built the Birkenhead Iron Works in 1824 and upon being joined by his son John the two turned their attention to shipbuilding in 1829. William Laird had a plan for the area and commissioned an Edinburgh architect called Gillespie Graham to put this into practice. This took the form of Hamilton Square and a series of broad avenues radiating from it, forming a neat grid pattern.

In 1841 William passed away and his role in the business and local affairs was largely taken up by his son John. Along with another businessman named William Jackson, the two set out to develop the town further, laying out important public buildings and areas such as Birkenhead Park. They also drew up plans for the dock system that was constructed around the former Wallasey Pool.

By 1877 a charter of incorporation as a Municipal Borough was granted, followed eleven years later by County Borough status. The town's coat of arms can be seen above. The symbols reflect the different

parts of the borough, with the crosier and single lion representing Birkenhead town, the oak comes from Tranmere, and the two lions from Oxton. The motto "Ubi Fides Ibi Lux Et Robur" means "Wherever there is faith, there is also light and strength".

The population at this time was 99,000 people, quite a jump form 1800 when it stood at 110! Part of this was because of the influx of people coming to work in the town, using the trains and steam ferries to commute. Birkenhead had also grown in area, and by 1877 included the town centre, Tranmere, Claughton, Oxton and Rock Ferry. Further growth in 1928 and 1933 added Prenton, Landican, Thingwall, Bidston, Noctorum, Upton, Arrowe and Woodchurch.

During the war arguably the borough's biggest contribution to the war effort was the work of the Cammell Laird shipyards. The yards' role in helping win victory began long before the war, with Birkenhead-built warships fighting in many different theatres. Three of these (HMS *Prince of Wales*, HMS *Ark Royal* and HMS *Nelson*) played crucial roles in the sinking of the German battleship *Bismarck* for example.

During the war the yard turned out a total of 106 fighting ships, an astonishing average of one every twenty days. It also put in sterling work repairing damaged vessels, patching up 9 battleships, 11 aircraft carriers and 100 other warships. For the repair work on two of the battleships the yards' workers received a special commendation from the Admiralty. Winston Churchill also visited the yards

(below) on at least one occasion to inspect work there and help keep up the morale of the work force.

The borough suffered heavily for its role in the war effort, with 442 people killed and 606 seriously wounded. The worst month was March 1941 when almost half of those casualties occurred, and nearly as many people were killed in Birkenhead as the rest of Merseyside put together. It also lost 2079 houses that were completely destroyed and had a further 26,000 damaged.

Like the rest of the region these numbers would have been much higher had it not been for the sterling efforts of the men, women and children of the borough who volunteered to work in the Civil Defence organisations.

This photograph shows the premises of Hubbard and Martin, a firm of bakers which stood on Pilgrim Street close to its junction with Chester Street. The damage seen here was done on the night of 12/13 March 1941, but fortunately no-one was killed in this area. The ornate street lamp on the left stood outside the Pilgrim Street Elementary School. Not far from here is Monks Ferry, site of a medieval crossing point to Liverpool. The name derives from the fact that it was originally operated by monks attached to the nearby Benedictine Priory. They had been granted a royal licence to do so in 1330, but lost it after Henry VIII's Dissolution of the Monasteries. The ferry ceased operation in 1878 with Woodside Ferry taking most of its business. A nearby railway station also known as Monks Ferry was in operation from 1844 to the 1960s, although it closed to passengers in 1878 and by the time of the war was only open to goods traffic.

The premises of Hubbard and Martin are still intact and remain largely unchanged. They are currently home to an engineering firm. Although the lamp post has long since been removed the school is still here, but is now known as Gilbrook Special School.

Birkenhead Priory is still standing, making it the oldest building in Merseyside. In its grounds is the tomb of John Laird, often considered to be the most important person in the history of Birkenhead. It is fitting that his final resting place is so close to the shipyard which he helped to develop.

Hamilton Square was laid out in 1826 on land bought by William Laird, the Scottish shipbuilder who did so much to develop the town. Most of the buildings were completed over the next twenty years, with the Town Hall (the building with the clock tower on the right) completing the set in 1887. The terraced buildings that form the square were originally intended as houses, with the open space in the foreground laid out as gardens. In 1903 the gardens were bought by the Council and opened to the public. In the centre background is the cenotaph, erected after World War One. The position of the cenotaph caused controversy as it was formerly the site of a statue of John Laird. This was moved to the opposite side of the square and positioned with his back to the Town Hall, which some people felt was inappropriate. Just above the Georgian buildings on the left the brick tower of Hamilton Square Station can just be made out, along with a chimney poking up behind it. Birkenhead is rather fortunate that this particular bomb landed in the gardens, and not on any of the fine Georgian buildings that surround it!

The majority of the buildings in the square are now office premises. The former gardens are still open to the public and contain a monument to Queen Victoria in the style of a cross. In addition to the cenotaph, that area of the square contains a number of memorial plaques to different services who saw action during wartime. The tower above the station remains. Originally this would have contained a hydraulic system to operate the lifts, similar to one that was once used at James Street Station in Liverpool. This modern view was taken from a different angle as trees and bushes blocked a direct comparison.

Taken in Hamilton Street, this image shows the devastation inflicted on W. M. Bernard's, a firm of Ironmongers which was hit on the night of 1/2 October 1940. Next door on the left was the premises of the *Birkenhead Advertiser*, a newspaper that produced its first edition in 1853. The building on the far left once housed a free library, but services moved to the new central library in Borough Road in 1934.

Neither the buildings nor paper have survived the passage of time. The site is now occupied by Land Registry offices.

This photograph shows the stables of Yate's Castle Brewery, which were on the corner of Chester Street and Water Street. The main local offices for the brewery were in Hamilton Street, although it was a Manchester-based firm. Their local pubs included the Windsor Castle Hotel which is on Oxton Road, Birkenhead, a short distance from the Victoria Vaults on page 82. As can be seen elsewhere in the book horse driven transport was still used throughout Merseyside during this period and the war greatly increased this. When it came to the clearing and removal efforts though lorries such as the one on the right were often used to speed efforts. This area was especially important as Chester Street is very close to Hamilton Square Station, Woodside Station and the Cammell Laird shipyards. The damage seen here was done on the night of 12/13 March 1941, although fortunately no-one seems to have been killed here. A short distance from Water Street was a series of graving docks known as Clover's which were owned by the firm of Grayson Rollo. The firm's premises on the far side of the Mersey at Sandhills and in South Liverpool were also damaged.

The stables have been cleared and replaced with modern business premises and a car park, although there are plans to build modern apartments on the latter. The graving docks were later owned by a firm called Western Ship Repairers, but they closed in the 1980s and the docks have since been filled in. They are now the site of apartments and offices.

Located at number 63 Argyle Street was the Boilermakers Hall, a branch of an international club for trades people involved in various aspects of shipbuilding. In the case of this branch many of its members would have been employed at the nearby Cammell Laird shipyards. Argyle Street was hit several times during the raids and although the photograph remains undated, an educated guess can be taken as to when the building was hit. This photograph was almost certainly taken a day or two after a raid since there has been no attempt to make the site safe, despite the interior clearly being dangerous. This suggests a busy night, of which Birkenhead suffered several. The first time the street was hit was on the night of 26/27 September 1940 when the Argyle Theatre was damaged. On 1/2 October 1940 bombs landed in the street and the civil defence workers had to use their gas masks due to the damage causing a leak from the mains. On the night of 13/14 October however, one of the buildings known to have been hit was the Savoy Cinema, which at number 53 was quite close to the Boilermakers Hall. This makes it quite likely that the photograph was taken in mid October 1940.

The pre-war building has long since been replaced by this modern equivalent of a similar size and layout. On the far left of the photograph can be seen the side wall of the former Savoy Cinema. It closed in March 1982 and was later converted into a snooker hall.

one of the most important theatres outside of London. Some indication of its status can be seen from the list of famous stars that played here, which included George Formby, Stan Laurel, Eric Morecambe, Ernie Wise and Charlie Chaplin. George Formby was ignominiously booed offstage on his first appearance here, but was an extremely popular performer during the war years. In 1896 the theatre put on a show of what was then described as "living pictures", making it the Wirral's first cinema. This may even have been the first time they were shown anywhere in the country outside of London. Further achievements followed, with it hosting the first broadcast direct to radio in 1931, and shortly after it became the first theatre to broadcast directly to America. Sadly the bombs put a stop to all this, reducing much of the interior to a charred ruin, although some of the decorative panels on the balconies survived

As mentioned on the previous page, the Argyle Theatre was struck by incendiary bombs on the night of 26/27 September 1940. The interior of the building was completely burnt out, collapsing the ceiling and roof into the seating area below. The building first opened its doors as the Argyle Music Hall in 1868 and during its lifetime was considered

With so many achievements to its name it is disappointing to discover that the theatre never re-opened. Although the interior had been gutted, the exterior survived largely intact and was used for many years as storage, before eventually being demolished. The site is now used as a car park for a nearby department store.

The Queensway Tunnel was begun in 1925, took nine years to complete and cost £8 million. For the first 24 years of its existence it was the longest underwater tunnel in the world. This photograph shows the view from near the branch tunnel rather than the main entrance. This lead out onto Rendel Street and was generally used by people travelling to the docks or Wallasey. On the night of 24/25 June 1941 high explosive bombs landed on Perrin's Stables, killing nine horses and blocking the entrance to the tunnel. As the tunnel was a crucial transport artery for the region, workers were able to quickly clear the blockage (as can be seen in the photograph) and allow transport to use it once more.

After the war the decline in importance of the docks, combined with the proposal to open a second tunnel connecting Wallasey to Liverpool meant that the Birkenhead Branch Tunnel fell out of use, closing in 1965. This modern comparison had to be taken from road level as modern buildings blocked a direct comparison.

The shattered buildings in this photograph stood between 63 and 67 Watson Street. The building on the far right was Maypole's Dairy Company. Next to this stood Alfred Foster's fishmongers shop. The bomb that caused this damage seems to have struck this building, since rubble and wooden beams have crashed down into the adjacent Oak Street. On the far side of Oak Street, the building nearest to the camera was occupied by Oliver Neligan's fish and chips shop. Watson street was targeted three times during the raids, on the nights of 21/22 December 1940, 12/13 February 1941 and 12/13 March 1941. The damage seen here was done during the third raid. The only fatality in the street that night was Eliza Watson who was killed at number 52. No-one else was killed in the street on the other nights, although the damage was fairly widespread as can be seen below.

This photograph shows the remains of the Caledonian Hotel, which stood on the corner of Cleveland Street and Cathcart Street. The severe damage seen here was done on the night of 13 March 1941. In all there were eleven deaths at this location that night. Aileen Jones and her parents Elsie and William died alongside the Summer family which consisted of Peter and Catherine, along with their children Ann, Anthony, Kathleen and Marie. The final two deaths were Annie Jones and William Parry. Just a short distance along Cleveland Street from here once stood the works of the Starbuck Factory. This was the site of the first tramcar factory in the whole of Europe. Between 1862 and 1913 the factory turned out around 3000 trams for both the UK and overseas markets. Some of these are still used today in places like the Isle of Man. Along with George Train, George Starbuck helped promote trams as a means of transport. By the outbreak of war though the premises had been taken over by a carpet cleaning company. On the other side of the road from this factory was the Corporation depot which housed the cleaning and transport departments.

Since the war a car sales and car wash premises were erected on the site of the Caledonian Hotel.

George Starbuck's former factory is now a home appliance sales room, with only a small plaque on the outside of the building to remind passers-by of its importance. The depot remains largely unchanged although it is now managed by the Corporation's successor, Wirral Borough Council.

Livingstone Street runs between Park Road North and Corporation Road. It was named after the famous Scottish Missionary who spent half of his life exploring Africa. The ship he used to navigate one of that continent's rivers was built in the Laird Brothers' yard, and he visited the town in 1858 to see it under construction. This section of the street stood between Payson Street and Beckwith Street. The damage seen here could have been done on one of four separate nights, but the most likely would have been 25/26 September 1940. On this night two people were killed at number 119 Livingstone Street. Elizabeth Oxton was aged seventy three, whereas Maureen Ledsom was only three years old. Sad proof of how the raids were indiscriminate, with no one age group spared or targeted. Although number 119 house stood on the far side of Beckwith Street from here, the damage could easily have occurred at the same time. Livingstone Street also suffered raids on the nights of 31 August/1 September 1940, 1/2 October 1940 and 1/2 November 1941. Not far away, on Park Road North was the Borough Hospital which was hit on the night of 12/13 March 1941. Although the operating theatre was struck, the building wasn't too badly damaged and remained in use.

Modern houses occupy this section of Livingstone Street. Payson Street no longer exists but would have stood to the left of these houses. The site of the Borough Hospital is also now occupied by modern housing.

Price Street Police Station was located at the corner of Price Street and Livingstone Street. This particular photograph, taken shortly after the raids on the night of 13/14 March 1941 shows the entrance on Livingstone Street. The building has had most of its windows shattered and some damage to the roof, but is mostly intact, as is the public shelter on the right. The sandbags in front of the building would have been placed there to protect it from blast damage in future raids. Price Street is one of many long straight roads in this part of Birkenhead which was laid out in the kind of grid system that is common to many American cities. In the background on the left are the public baths. Public baths were a common sight on Merseyside and many served as both swimming pools and a place where people could go for a wash. Often they would also include attached laundry facilities. This may seem like a strange concept to a modern society used to central heating, washing machines and showers, but they played an important role in Victorian efforts to improve the health of the working class populations of towns and cities. Although things had improved somewhat since Victorian times, many houses retained the likes of outside toilets until well into the twentieth century.

The public baths were demolished in the early 1970s and have been replaced by a children's playground. The Police Station has also been demolished since the war, with the site now occupied by modern housing.

Located just off Duke Street, Harcourt Street was struck on the night of 12/13 March 1941, Birkenhead's worst night. At number 40 Joseph Tucker, a 64 year old shipwright was critically injured in the raid. Rescued from his house, he was taken to Birkenhead General Hospital, but sadly died there on the 13th. Number 40 would have been the second house in the row that juts out slightly further than the buildings nearest to the camera. Another victim of that night's raid was Edward Price, a 63 year old man who lived some distance away in Park Road East. One of the street's residents was also the victim of an earlier night's action. James Forshaw, who lived an number 20 had been killed at the Corporation Bus Depot at Laird Street on 21 December 1940. The building in the foreground on the left was a fruit sellers belonging to Frank Johnson. On the other corner of Duke Street and Harcourt Street was a branch of Irwins, a large grocery company. The advertising sign on the side of this building is for Capstan cigarettes, a brand that has been produced since 1894.

All of the houses in this part of Harcourt Street are still standing. Frank Johnson's fruit shop seems to have been demolished since the war and replaced with this modern building. Capstans are still sold, but recent laws have severely restricted the way in which tobacco in all its forms is advertised, making such huge billboards a thing of the past.

The building in the centre of this photograph is the remains of Birkenhead Park Station. The damage occurred during the night of 12/13 March 1941, Birkenhead's worst raid as nearly 300 people died and a similar number were injured. Located on Duke Street, Birkenhead Park Station was opened in 1888 and provided a link between the Mersey Railway to Liverpool and the Wirral Railway which ran to West Kirby. There is a certain irony in the sign in the centre of Duke Street about no smoking since the only other visible sign on the left is advertising Will's Gold Flake, a type of cigarette popular during the war. The badly damaged premises to which it was attached was a tobacconists called Finlay and Co. To the left of this was a branch of the Birkenhead and District Co-Operative Society who also had premises a little further along Duke Street.

Since the war this area has undergone considerable change. Still open today, Birkenhead Park Station provides links to New Brighton, West Kirby and Liverpool. The station building was rebuilt after the war in its current functional style. In the background can be seen two examples of post war housing that replaced those seen in the wartime image, a block of flats on the left and some more modern apartment buildings on the right. The only remaining building that has not altered a great deal since the war is the premises of the Co-Operative Society, although they no longer occupy it.

seven fatalities and Old Bidston Road another two. At number 479 Price Street five members of the same extended family fell, their ages ranging between nine and thirty six. The father, Arthur Sherlock ran a fish and chip shop at that address, and was sadly cut down in his prime alongside his wife Winifred and their children Hilda, William and Bernard. Other victims in Price Street that night were John Hopkins who lived in Livingstone Street, and George Young who lived some distance away in Moreton. George's presence can be explained by the fact that he was a firewatcher assigned to duties in the nearby Birkenhead and District Co-Operative Society's boot repairing depot. It is quite likely that he was an employee of the firm. Further along Old Bidston Road at number 122 two ladies were killed, Ada Lowe and Violet Blythe.

Located at the corner of Price Street (in the foreground) and Old Bidston Road (out of shot on the left), the Canada Hotel was a victim of the raid on the night of 12/13 March 1941. Devastated though the building was, no-one was killed here that night. Unfortunately other nearby residents were not so lucky, with Price Street the scene of

The Canada Hotel and all the houses which stood to its right have been pulled down, their place taken by a school playground. Both 471 and 479 Price Street were a short distance to the left of where this photograph was taken. Number 122 Old Bidston Road was further down the road, its site now covered by the school's buildings.

This photograph shows Our Lady's Roman Catholic church which stood on the corner of Cavendish Street and Price Street, although this view was taken from the rear of the building in St Mary's Street. The church and its adjoining presbytery were hit on the night of 12/13 March 1941 and sadly Canon Tallon was killed. Also killed at the Presbytery that night was Catherine Ryan, whilst in nearby St Mary's Street George Smith was killed. In the foreground viewing the damage are three dignitaries, including what would appear to be two mayors. During the war Wallasey, Birkenhead and Bebington all had separate councils with their own mayor. Not far away from here is the Vittoria Dock which was finished in 1909. Shortly before completion in March a temporary dam which was holding back the water from where the labourers were excavating collapsed, killing fourteen of the workers. Between 1937 and 1941 a nineteenth century training ship named HMS *Conway* was stationed in the dock, but with the increasing air raids on the region she was moved to a mooring in North Wales, on the Anglesey side of the Menai Straits.

The church was repaired after the war and remains in use today. Modern buildings make a direct comparison impossible, so this view shows the front of the building from Cavendish Street. In 1953 HMS *Conway* ran aground in the Menai Strait as she was on her way back to Birkenhead for a refit. The damage was too great for her to be moved and she later caught fire, destroying most of the remains. Her place in Vittoria Dock is now occupied by HMS *Plymouth*, a Falklands War era Frigate that was once on display alongside *U534* (see page 10).

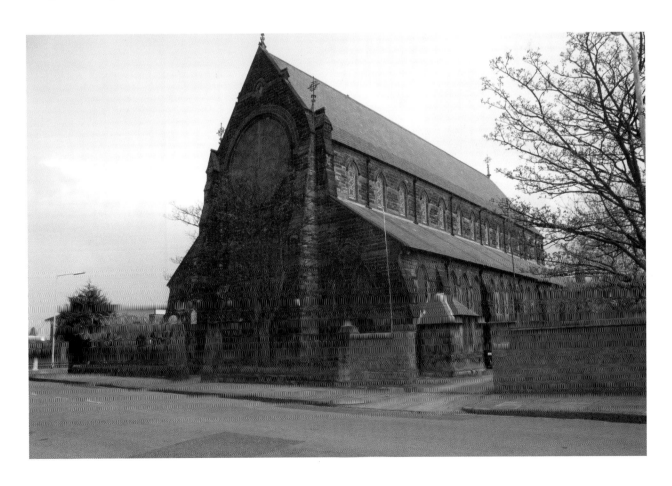

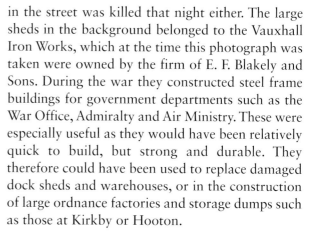

This photograph shows Severn Street, which ran between Buccleuch Street and Lincoln Street. Given its close proximity to the West Float it will come as no surprise to learn that most of the residents of this street listed their occupation as labourer, seaman or dock labourer. The houses seen here suffered damage during a raid on the night of 21/22 December 1940, although none of them seem to have been too badly hit. The residents could consider themselves doubly fortunate since no-one in the street was killed that night either. The large sheds in the background belonged to the Vauxhall Iron Works, which at the time this photograph was taken were owned by the firm of E. F. Blakely and Sons. During the war they constructed steel frame buildings for government departments such as the War Office, Admiralty and Air Ministry. These were especially useful as they would have been relatively quick to build, but strong and durable. They therefore could have been used to replace damaged dock sheds and warehouses, or in the construction of large ordnance factories and storage dumps such as those at Kirkby or Hooton.

Although the houses undoubtedly survived the war they have since been demolished, and Severn Street exists only as a broad tarmac path through wasteland. The Vauxhall Ironworks buildings are still standing and even today are still occupied by a steel fabrication company.

The missing houses in the centre of the photograph are numbers 62-68 Laird Street. On the night of 12/13 March 1941, Laird Street was devastated by a group of land mines and high explosive bombs that landed at various points along it. It's likely that the damage seen here was done by a bomb rather than a much more destructive land mine, as the latter generally had a much wider blast radius. No-one was killed in these houses that night, and it may well have been the owners who have added a defiant gesture to the shattered remains of their property. At the bottom of the roof that is hanging precariously down it is just possible to make out a Union flag with its distinctive stripes. The people of Birkenhead were determined to show, like so many across the region and country as a whole, that they could take whatever Hitler's Luftwaffe could throw at them. Other sections of Laird Street were not as lucky as this one. Much further along the road, the houses between numbers 316 and 330 (between Landsdowne Road and Vulcan Street) were all but flattened and more than 20 people died. Laird Street had also been hit on the night of 21/22 December 1940 when six people were killed by a bomb that fell on a tram shed shelter.

The land that the houses once occupied was never built on after the war. The gap they took up is now occupied by advertising hoardings.

This photograph was taken at the junction of Park Road North and Mallaby Street, looking towards Laird Street in the distance. In the foreground are two overturned buses and another two badly damaged ones are still standing a little further down the street. In this raid an estimated 136 buses were damaged, 8 of which were beyond repair. Although Birkenhead had seen the construction of Britain's first street tramway in 1860 (see page 49), by the 1930s buses had replaced trams on most routes and the last tram ran on 17 July 1937. Like Wallasey but unlike Liverpool therefore, Birkenhead's wartime transport system was more flexible. This made it less prone to problems caused by roads blocked by the rubble from demolished buildings. The chimney on the right probably belonged to the premises of the United Yeast Company, a firm of bakers who had their premises on Laird Street. Also on Laird Street, opposite the junction with Mallaby Street was the corporation bus depot, formerly a tramways depot. Seven men lost their lives at the depot when a shelter they were in received a direct hit.

Since the war the houses on the left hand side of Mallaby Street were for the most part patched up and repaired, but those on the right were rebuilt. The Corporation depot is still in use but is now owned by a private bus firm.

Located on a site at the corner of Norman Street and Bidston Avenue was the Avenue Cinema. It was officially opened in 1928 and had room for 1200 people. It was considered quite advanced for its time, with floodlights attached to the building in order to illuminate its own dedicated car park. The cinema's name was also illuminated by 166 flashing red and white lamps. This particular scene of destruction shows the main entrance on the Norman Street side of the building after damage done in the raid on the night of 12/13 March 1941. Two people fell victim to the bombs in the street that night. Josiah Williams, a 37 year old who lived in nearby Clifford Street was killed instantly. William Thomas, a 43 year old ARP warden who lived at number 48 Norman Street (further up the road, between the junctions with Elfet Street and Upper Brassey Street) was injured and taken to the Birkenhead Municipal Hospital in Church Street. Sadly he passed away on 4 April 1941.

Although the damage to the Avenue looks contained to a fairly small area of the building, the wartime photograph does not tell the whole story. The

cinema's foundations were badly damaged and irreparable, leaving the structure unsafe. It was eventually demolished to make way for the Avenue public house which can be seen on the left. This has also closed in recent times and the future of the site remains uncertain.

Mona Street runs just off Alderley Avenue, close to its junction with Upton Road. On the night of 12/13 March 1941 several high explosive bombs landed here, killing two people, William Aspinall, who was aged 34 and James Collins who was aged 40. What is unusual about this is that neither man lived in the street at the time of the raid. William lived in St James Gardens, and James lived in Landsdowne Place. Exactly what brought these men to meet their fate in this short street that night is unknown. It is possible that they were staying with friends or relatives. Since neither were listed as members of the civil defence services they may simply have been unlucky enough to be passing through the area that night. Other photos taken at the same time show a rather strange aspect of the effects of bombing. The bricks on the upper floor of the second house on the left have held together, but that section looks as if it has been bent backwards, almost as easily as someone would fold a piece of paper. It's also worth noting the criss-cross pattern on the windows of the houses on the left. This used tape to try and prevent the window from shattering into tiny pieces and showering people inside with flying glass. This was a quick, cheap and easy alternative to erecting shuttering, especially during wartime when vital resources such as wood and metal were in especially short supply.

Mona Street remains largely the same today, with all the damaged houses repaired in the same style. No trace is left of the devastation the residents saw when they opened their front doors.

This was the scene that greeted the residents of Daffodil Road, Claughton on 22 December 1940. The night's raiders had dropped a high explosive bomb squarely on top of number 32, reducing it to a sea of rubble and damaging the houses on either side. Joseph Jones (53), his wife Elizabeth (42) and their daughter Gwyneth (20) were killed in the raid. No-one else was killed in the road that night. Daffodil Road was also hit in a raid on 12/13 March 1941 when number 9 (below right) was damaged. Fortunately all of the road's residents survived this second raid. Not far from here is Flaybrick Hill Cemetery, the oldest public cemetery on the Wirral. It opened in 1864 and contains over 100,000 burials. Many of the victims of the air raids were laid to rest here. There was also once an infectious diseases hospital nearby. Since the raid number 32 has been rebuilt and number 9 repaired, leaving no trace of the effect Hitler's bombers had on this part of the borough. The infectious diseases hospital was renamed St James' Hospital in 1948 but was demolished in the 1990s. A housing estate now stands on its site.

Another of Birkenhead's long roads is Upton Road. On the night of 1/2 May 1941 several high explosive bombs landed there, damaging the two houses seen above. On the left is number 125, known as Heathbank, whilst on the right is 127 known as Tredinnock. Three nights later Intabene (below), which stands on the other side of the road was also hit and suffered slight damage. No-one was killed in either raid, but a 29 year old woman called Elizabeth Hunt who lived at number 11a had been killed on the night of 18 October 1940.

Number 127 was rebuilt in exactly the same style, whereas Intabene and number 125 were repaired. Although it retains the same appearance, Intabene is now subdivided into flats and impossible to see from the road.

Several houses in St David Road in Claughton were hit during the raid on the night of 1/2 May 1941. The photograph above left shows damage done to numbers 17-19, whilst below the damage done to numbers 9-15 can be seen. The ARP wardens have erected barriers across the road to warn civilians of the danger ahead. One of these can just be seen in the photograph below as a bomb has left a large crater in the centre of the road. This would be a hazard for pedestrians and vehicles alike, especially at night when the blackout was in force.

Despite the extensive damage to the road and walls surrounding the houses, there was no loss of life in the road that night and all of the buildings were repaired, leaving no trace of the damage today.

This photograph shows on the right the remains of the garage attached to 30 Beryl Road, Noctorum. The road was struck twice during the war. The first raid on the night of 28/29 May 1941 dropped only oil bombs on the road. Although they could be potentially dangerous, these could be dealt with without too much difficulty by the residents themselves. The second raid on the night of 20/21 October 1941 was more serious. A parachute mine fell in a field near the road, blasting a large crater 30ft wide and 15ft deep. Four soldiers (possibly from a disposal squad) were injured in the blast but fortunately no-one was killed. The significance of the letters "SP" on the fence surrounding number 30 is unknown. Not far away was the Kielberg Convalescent Home which was also hit. The home was associated with the Children's Hospital on Woodchurch Road. It was built with money donated by a Danish born businessman called Sir Michael Ferdinand Krøyer-Kielberg, who lived for a time in Liverpool and was married in Wallasey. Although he had become a British subject in 1926, he retained strong links to the country of his birth. During the war he promoted the Free Denmark

Movement which aimed to help liberate that country from Nazi occupation.

Number 30's garage has been completely rebuilt since the war. The convalescent home is no longer standing, its site occupied in part by modern housing.

This photograph (below left) shows 32 Manor Drive in Upton. The house was hit during the night of 28/29 May 1941 by a high explosive bomb which opened it up like a child's doll house. Rather amazingly several items of furniture can be seen largely intact but teetering on the edge of the gaping hole where there was once a wall. Manor Drive had also been hit earlier in the month when the nearby Heath Drive was struck as well (bottom), with numbers 30, 32 and 34 demolished. Another bomb landed just outside the nearby Upton Railway Station. None of the damage done in these photographs lead to any deaths, although they must have caused considerable disruption.

The modern photograph shows that number 32 was rebuilt after the war, as were all of the houses on Heath Drive. The nearby station remains open.

Woodchurch Road is one of Birkenhead's longest, running all the way from a junction with Balls Road to Arrowe Park. This particular image is of the houses either side of number 425 which were slightly damaged on the night of 5/6 May 1941. Around the same time a bomb landed in nearby Carlaw Road (below right), causing light damage to number 38. The residents of these houses could consider themselves especially lucky since not only did they escape the raids with their lives, the damage to their houses was slight enough that it could be repaired relatively easily.

As you would expect all of the houses seen in these photographs are still standing, with even the damage done to the walls repaired. The building on the far right (which is on the corner of Woodchurch Road and Osmaston Road) is now occupied by a residential home.

Taken at the opposite end of Waterpark Road from the photograph on page 70 (close to the junction with Storeton Road), this image shows the damage from a high explosive bomb that has landed near number 12, damaging the perimeter wall and cratering the road in the foreground. Number 10 was also damaged, as were Norcroft (below) and Oakdene which stand on the opposite side of the road. The local residents were lucky as this near miss caused no deaths. The archive records do not state on what date this damage was done, and since the road was hit on several different nights the exact date proved impossible to track down.

Apart from some minor cosmetic changes all the houses in this part of the road remain standing.

This photograph shows 14 Prenton Lane, also known as Quantea. On the night of 8/9 August 1940, the night of the first bombing raid on Birkenhead, a bomb fell through the hole in the roof seen here and killed a maid called Johanna Mandale. She was the first fatality on Merseyside. The house belonged to a Mr Walter Bunney who owned the famous Bunney's department store which stood at the corner of Whitechapel and Church Street in Liverpool. Also

badly damaged in the same raid was another nearby house known as Ardock (below) and the war memorial (see next page)

Although the building was still empty and in need of repair by 1944, it is still standing today. The growth of foliage and considerations of privacy meant that the comparison photograph was taken from the opposite side of the road.

This photograph shows the aftermath of the raid on 2/3 May 1941 on part of Prenton Lane. In the foreground can be seen the Prenton War Memorial. Behind it on the left can be seen a house known as Hillside, whilst on the right is Braeside. The war memorial was erected in 1919 and dedicated to the people of Prenton who lost their lives in what was then known as the Great War, but we now call World War One. There was also a second, separate stone erected here in recognition of the services of the Mercantile Marine during the same conflict. Fortunately despite the considerable damage no-one was killed in Hillside, which at the time was owned by George Stavely, a cotton broker.

The memorial was badly damaged and had to be rebuilt after the war. The growth of trees and bushes in the background makes it hard to tell, but Hillside was demolished after the war and a new house was built on the site. The war memorial forms a focus point for modern Remembrance Days, which are held on the second Sunday in November. Members of the local community, veterans and local church members gather here and there is a one minute silence in memory of all those who have been killed in conflicts since World War One. Similar events occur throughout the region.

On the night of 5/6 May 1941 high explosive bombs landed in Prenton Hall Road in Prenton. The building seen on the right was amongst those in the area that suffered damage, but fortunately no-one was killed in the road that night. The road had also been struck by bombs earlier in the week, but the residents' luck held and there was not a single fatality then either. The building stands opposite the junction with Waterpark Road and served as a cottage for staff working at the local waterworks. This consisted of a huge central building, which housed pumping engines for what is known as the Prenton Borehole. The original coal driven system was apparently incredibly noisy, but effective. The road itself was named after Prenton Hall which in fact stands a short distance away at the corner of Prenton Dell Road and Prenton Dell Avenue.

In the 1970s the authorities decided they would replace the ageing and outdated waterworks machinery with a new electrical pumping system. This is housed on the same site, but in a smaller building, and is no doubt much quieter! The original main building was demolished, but the subject of our photograph survived. For a time it was used by the Water Board for storing equipment, but it is now a private residence known as Springwater Cottage. A modern wall and hedge now blocks a proper comparison. Prenton Hall is also still standing, although it has long since been incorporated into a large farm house.

Running roughly parallel to Woodchurch Road, Holm Lane was hit on the night of 7/8 April 1941. The houses seen here ran between numbers 128 and 120. Holm Lane was also the site of an anti-aircraft battery. Many of the crews of these guns worked long hours to provide one of the region's main defences against the Luftwaffe's bombers. The guns were not universally liked however since some of the larger calibre varieties made a lot of noise and the vibration from firing the shells shook the nearby houses, often damaging windows and ceilings. Once the raids started though the guns remained the most visible and audible evidence that the locals had not been abandoned to their fate. Holm Lane was just one of many roads in Oxton that were damaged during the war, which left a total of 82 houses completely demolished and a further 492 severely damaged. The residents here escaped the raid without any fatalities. At the far end of Holm Lane is Ingestre Road. In the grounds of a large house on that road was found a polished stone axe that dated back to the Neolithic period of pre-history. This along with a Bronze Age axe found not far away in Noctorum Way shows that the region has been settled for thousands of years. Until recently however much of the land was owned by the Earls of Shrewsbury, which accounts for the numerous roads nearby named in honour of the various titles the earls earned, such as Wexford Road and Talbot Road.

As might be expected, the houses in this area of Holm Lane were repaired to their pre-war condition.

The rubble in the centre of this photograph is all that remained of Caernarvon Castle public house in Bidston Road, Oxton after the raid of 12/13 March 1941. There were two fatalities here that night. John Trenholm who was aged 58 was the landlord of the pub. The second fatality, Ernest Hopkins was 38 and lived in nearby Claughton. A short distance further up Bidston Road at number 45 was the early headquarters of the Birkenhead Battalion of the Local Defence Volunteers (later renamed the Home Guard). The battalion used the billiard room of H. Russell Edward's house for a time before moving to a Territorial Army drill hall in Grange Road West, then finally to a large house in Devonshire Place once used by the Army. Just out of shot on the right is St Saviour's church, completed in 1892. The raid destroyed the stained glass windows in the church, but left the main structure largely intact.

The modern day Caernarvon Castle was rebuilt further back from the road, allowing for a car park at the front of the building. The building on the right has gone. St Saviour's is still standing, its windows repaired. There is also a memorial to the members of the parish who fell in both World Wars that was designed by Giles Gilbert Scott, architect of Liverpool's Anglican Cathedral.

St Aidan's Theological College was founded in 1846 by the Reverend Joseph Baylee, the Vicar of Holy Trinity church on Price Street. The building stood on Shrewsbury Road, not far from its junction with Tollemache Road. Facing it is this large Victorian terrace, named after the college. The photograph was undated, but it would be reasonable to assume that the damage seen here was done during the night of 21/22 December 1940. At this time damage had been done to numbers 91-95 Shrewsbury Road (below) which were just opposite the college and terrace.

The terrace fortunately survived the raids, as did the college. The latter was closed in 1969 and was demolished a year later. The site is now occupied by St Aidan's Court.

The Civil Defence workers seen in this photograph are sifting through the rubble of what was once numbers 30 and 32 St Vincent Road, Claughton on 2 May 1941. The presence of so many workers is probably due to local people knowing just how many people may have been buried somewhere in the rubble, dead or alive. Even though it may seem hopeless to our untrained eyes, the workers would often pull people alive from the wreckage of their homes, sometimes many hours later. Sadly their efforts at this location would largely be in vain for at least eight people were killed at this address the night before. At number 30 Joseph Cashin (63) and his daughter Margaret Cashin (33) were killed. At number 32 two families and an individual were victims of the raid. Mary Platt and her two sons, Harry (15) and William (18) fell, alongside Ida Powell (38), her son John (18) and daughter Patricia (5). Margaret Dommett (42), a woman listed as living at number 32 was also named as being killed in the street that night, but strangely not at the house. The final victim was Francis Pursall (40) who lived in St Anne Street but died somewhere in this street. The house was listed in pre-war directories as being occupied by Hugh Platt and his family. This suggests that the Powell family and Margaret

Dommett may have been staying at the house temporarily, perhaps after being bombed out of their own home in an earlier raid.

After the war both houses were rebuilt in a style that so closely matches those around them that it is impossible to tell the difference.

This photograph shows the damage that has been done to houses and business premises in Devonshire Road, Claughton on the night of 12/13 March 1941. The buildings in the foreground were owned by George Bolton, who operated a garage and taxi firm from here. In the background on the right the rear of houses on Grosvenor Road can be seen. Fortunately the damage to this area appears to have been very slight and no-one was killed in the immediate vicinity. A short distance further down Devonshire Road stood St Mark's church which was consecrated in 1891. The church contained a "Father Willis" organ, which was made by the Liverpool-based firm of Henry Willis and Sons. The company were world leaders in their field and provided organs for town halls, cathedrals and churches around the world.

With the exception of some modern buildings that are blocking the view towards Grosvenor Road, the modern photograph shows that very little has changed in the intervening seven decades. St Mark's church closed in 1991 and despite it having been granted listed status it was demolished shortly after. Fortunately the organ was saved and later purchased by a private collector. He hopes to restore it to its former glory and install it in a cathedral in The Netherlands. Devonshire Road is named after the Dukes of Devonshire who employed Joseph Paxton as a head gardener. Paxton's connection to Birkenhead comes from the fact that he designed Birkenhead Park, which is not far to the north of here.

Located at the corner of Slatey Road and Mather Road this building was a Police Station. On the night of 28/29 of September 1940 a corner of the building was hit, leaving the gaping hole that appears on the far left. Although it may seem at first glance that the building was partly below street level this is in fact misleading. One attempt to protect buildings was to erect sandbags around them. This could only be done on the ground floor, as even the best stacked sandbags were liable to collapse in bad weather. Despite their name the sandbags would sometimes be filled with earth. Local people often volunteered to help fill the bags and there must have been tens of thousands of them used throughout the region.

The damage to the Police Station was repaired and the building survived the war, only to be demolished in 1989. The site now stands empty. On the far right the corner of the Williamson Art Gallery and Museum can just be seen. Built in 1928 it is named after John Williamson who was a Director of the Cunard Steamship Company, and his son Patrick. John bequeathed a considerable sum to support its construction. The museum houses large collections of shipbuilders' models (large scale models of the ship), many of which were built at the Cammell Laird shipyards. Important collections of porcelain, pottery and art are also held there. Fortunately the buildings survived the war without any significant damage, and the museum remains open today.

The policeman in the foreground is talking to someone in front of the remnants of number 16 Euston Grove, which was demolished during the raid on the night of 12/13 March 1941. The spire in the distance belongs to Christ Church. In total six people were killed in the vicinity that night. At number 16 Fanny Manthorpe (84), Francis Manthorpe (54) and Ada Rudd (55) fell. At number 20 the victims were two sisters, Evelyn and Winifred Maddock (53 and 52 respectively). At the far end of this block of houses, on the corner with Mather Road May Evans (55) was killed at number 24. On the far side of the road numbers 15-21 were also badly damaged (below), although no-one was killed there.

After the war the entire block of houses were rebuilt in a modern style.

On the night of 5/6 May 1941 bombs landed in the area around 29 Kings Mount, causing the damage seen above. On the same night number 13 Bessborough Road (which is at the top of King's Mount and is seen below right) was also damaged, possibly by bombs dropped by the same raider. No-one was killed by the raid in either road. This was not the first time that the area had come under attack, as on the night of 9/10 January that year

Bessborough Road was badly damaged. Seventy three year old Clement Hancock was killed at number 22 and two houses had to be demolished. A further 17 suffered major damage but were repairable.

After the war number 29 seems to have been rebuilt at some stage, whereas number 13 was completely repaired.

Just off Woodchurch Road is Bennetts Hill. On the night of 2/3 May 1941 this whole area was plastered with high explosive bombs, damaging houses on both sides of the road. Above are shown the houses between numbers 15 and 19, whereas the photograph below shows the shattered remains of number 12 in the foreground and numbers 14-20 beyond it. Despite the widespread damage no-one was actually killed in the road that night, although the residents suffered one loss. Beatrice McHutchon, a 60 year old woman who lived at number 8 was killed in the Woodchurch Road School shelter. Had she been at home that night it is unlikely that she would have survived as her house was completely demolished during the raid.

Most of the damaged houses were rebuilt after the war in a quite different style.

The men in this photograph are working on the rubble of two buildings that once stood on the corner of Woodville Road and Borough Road. They were demolished during the raid on the night of 12/13 March 1941. The nearest was the premises of Parkers, a fruit sellers, whilst next door was The Roscoe Radio Company. The surviving premises to the right were a newsagents belonging to Joseph Price, and Richard Hoyle's butcher's shop. Fortunately no-one was killed in the immediate vicinity during the raid. Other parts of Borough Road were not quite so lucky, with a total of ten of its residents falling victim to that night's raids. Like many of the kerbs around the borough, the lamppost has been painted with three white stripes to help drivers see it during the blackout. These blackout measures came into effect on 1 September 1940 (two days before war even broke out) and required local authorities and individuals to ensure that no lights were showing at night. The ARP wardens were responsible for ensuring that these rules were adhered to, and the government provided materials to ensure that householders could cover their windows and doors. The few vehicles still on the road had their lights fitted with special slotted covers to ensure that their light directed towards the ground. The authorities handed out strong fines to people caught breaking the rules.

None of the buildings mentioned above have survived to the modern day. Their place has been occupied in part by a grass embankment, with the area behind that taken up by a car spares business.

Brattan Road runs between Borough Road and Woodchurch Road. The road was utterly devastated by a land mine on the night of 12/13 March 1941 and thirteen people were killed. The mine landed not far away from where the photographer took this image, flattening the houses that stood in the foreground and out of shot on the right. It will come as little surprise to learn that all thirteen deaths occurred in this section of the road, with the youngest victim aged 17 and the oldest 76. In the background on the left can be seen part of Claughton Higher Grade School, whilst the buildings on in the background on the right are on the far side of Borough Road. Although probably taken the morning after the raid people are already at work trying to clear the rubble and perhaps search in vain for survivors, both of which must have seemed very daunting tasks at the time.

The houses on the left hand side of the road were never rebuilt and their site is now occupied by the modern Christ Church Primary School. The right hand side of Brattan Road (which was as badly damaged as the left) has been built up with modern housing.

On the night of 12/13 March 1941 a land mine landed in Oxton Road, smashing shops and properties in the area. The building in the centre of this photograph with the Bent's sign was the Victoria Vaults public house, known locally as "The Little House". The mine all but destroyed the interior of the pub and badly damaged the front wall of the building. The owner and his family were sheltering from the raid in the cellar, the entrance to which was blocked by falling rubble. Fortunately the family were saved by an ARP rescue squad who managed to clear a route to the chute that the brewers used to deliver barrels. A basic attempt has been made to secure the area by placing a temporary wooden barrier in front of the buildings. Sadly Lillian Robb, the 61 year old owner of the fish and chip shop to the left of the pub was not so lucky. She also chose to shelter in the cellar of her building, but the floor above collapsed in on her, killing her instantly. The building on the right was Thomas Griffith's butcher's shop. Nearby Carnforth Street (just out of shot on the right) suffered even

more damage, with half a dozen people killed on the same night. Oxton Road was also bombed on the night of 31 August/1 September 1940 when incendiary bombs landed on Rostances store, which stood at number 15.

None of the shops present in the wartime picture have survived and their site is now occupied by housing. Carnforth Street now only exists only in memory.

The Warwick Arms public house stood on the corner of Westbourne Road and Warwick Road. The former was twice struck by bombs during the war. On the night of 20/21 November 1940 no casualties were caused. Just over a month later on the night of 21/22 December, though, it was not so fortunate as a bomb landed somewhere in the road, critically injuring 39 year old Edith Halewood. Although she was taken to the Municipal Hospital on Church Street she died later on the 22nd. As she is only listed as being injured in the road rather than a specific location it is unknown what she was doing here that night, especially since she lived in Moon Street (some distance away off Exmouth Street). It is possible that she was on her way home or to a public shelter at the time and was unfortunate enough to be caught in the open when the bombs struck. The pub was the building on the left, and having borne the brunt of the damage, nearby residents would have to visit a new local for a little while! The signs around the window of the building next door refer to popular chocolate companies such as Fry's and Cadbury's. These remained popular despite the wartime rationing that made bars difficult to get hold of. On the far

left of the photograph the premises of James Sturgeon's grocer's shop can just be seen.

The Warwick Arms was rebuilt after the war and remains open to this day. Most of the remainder of this section of Westbourne Road has also changed, with modern housing replacing old. Warwick Road has been replaced by Warwick Close and no longer connects to Oxton Road.

This photograph was taken shortly after the night of 12/13 March 1941 near the junction of Borough Road, Austin Street and Clifton Crescent. The building on the far left was a newsagents. This was owned by William Smith and stood on the corner of the first two roads. To the right and slightly behind this is part of St Werburgh's Roman Catholic School, which stood on Clifton Crescent. A hastily erected barrier prevents vehicles from travelling any further along Clifton Crescent, perhaps due the road being cratered by one of the night's bombs. With petrol rationed and in such short supply, people who used bicycles to get around such as the man in the foreground were a common sight. For similar reasons many people used handcarts such

as the one by the barrier to carry away their belongings, or help clear away the rubble that the raids created.

This area of Birkenhead was significantly changed by the construction of a series of flyovers leading to and from the nearby Mersey Tunnel. This comparison was taken from beneath one of the flyovers. Most of the buildings in the wartime photograph have been swept away, revealing a view of St Werburgh's church in the centre of the image. The building on the far right is the Central Hotel. Austin Street no longer exists, its place now taken by a pedestrianised route to a part of the shopping area known as St Werburgh's Square.

These houses in Wheststone Lane were damaged by enemy action during the raid on the night of 12/13 March 1941. This photograph was probably taken a few days later as there has been enough time for the authorities to erect a warning barrier to prevent people from getting too close. No-one was killed in either building during the raid and although both have suffered broken windows and minor damage to the exterior brickwork, they seem structurally intact. Directly opposite these buildings stood the premises of Birkenhead YMCA which was founded in 1874, thirty years after the organisation was founded in London. The hostel provided rooms and meals for young men, and had special links to local firms such as Cammell Laird and the Blue Funnel Shipping Line. During the war many refugee survivors were housed in the hostel, so it is fortunate that it survived the raids intact. Birkenhead YMCA had a significant role to play in the development of the Scouting movement. Baden Powell, the movement's founder publicly inaugurated it in the YMCA's former premises in Grange Road, giving the 1st Birkenhead Scout Group a claim to being the oldest in the world. The YMCA moved to the Whetstone Lane area in 1935.

Both houses were repaired and remain standing today. The YMCA hostel that would have been so familiar to the refugees was demolished in recent years, to be replaced by new purpose built premises in 2007. Their former premises in Grange Road are now occupied by a clothing chain store.

Shaped like an inverted "R" Seymour Street in Tranmere runs from Church Road to Allerton Road. On the night of 6/7 May 1941 the street was hit by several high explosive bombs. One of the houses struck that night was number 36, which is pictured here. Although the house has clearly been severely damaged the residents survived the raid with no fatalities. This may well have been down to luck, but could just have easily have been due to the family using a shelter for protection. Large houses such as this one could probably afford to have their own Anderson Shelter erected in the garden, although there were also plenty of street shelters nearby. Not far from Seymour Street (on Church Road) is a hospital which was built between 1861 and 1863. It originally housed the Birkenhead Union Workhouse, but in 1934 became the Birkenhead Municipal Hospital. Many of those injured in the air raids would have been taken to this hospital, which housed over a thousand beds.

After the war modern supported living flats were constructed on the site of number 36. The Municipal Hospital was renamed St Catherine's Hospital in 1948, with control passing to the National Health Service at the same time. In more recent years it ceased to be a general hospital and specialises in geriatric and psychiatric patients. The buildings are now scheduled for transformation into a more modern community hospital.

Located at the foot of Hillside Road in Tranmere were the yards of David Williams, a fertilizer manufacturer. On the night of 6/7 May 1941 the entrance gates of the yard was damaged as one of a series of high explosive bomb landed in the area. Another bomb landed on the houses between 57 and 61 Hillside Road (right). Whilst it is possible that some people might have been injured here, there were no fatalities at either location.

The modern viewpoint looks towards the river, with the gates of the yard in the centre of the photograph. The large building in the background on the left is a covered construction hall for Cammell Laird Shipbuilders. The modern houses just visible on the right have replaced the wartime properties, including 57-61.

Located at the bottom of a steep hill, number 12 Holt Road was a victim of the raid on the night of 9/10 January 1941. A parachute mine landed on the road, doing so much damage to this building and the nearby Holt House that both had to be demolished shortly after. Elsewhere in the road numbers 14, 38 and all the houses between 5 and 35 had to be evacuated due to the considerable damage they had suffered. Somehow no-one was killed here that night. Close to Holt Road are the Tranmere Tunnels, a network of underground passageways cut into a rock outcrop to create a massive air raid shelter. First proposed at a council meeting in September 1940, they took a work force of over one hundred men more than two years to complete, by which time the raids on Merseyside were over! Eventually the tunnels had grown to such an extent that there was room for more than 6000 people and the complex included a canteen, toilets and a library. It cost £131,817 which was quite a large sum at the time.

The site of number 12 remains empty and overgrown to this day. The Tranmere Tunnels gradually fell out of use and at the end of the war were largely stripped of anything of value. They were then used for storage, before later being considered as a possible shelter for use in the event of a nuclear attack. Eventually they were abandoned and became a play area for the local children. The tunnels were sealed for good in 1989 to prevent the danger of children getting lost in the murky darkness and injuring themselves.

If any photograph demonstrates how much access the company of Stewart Bale Ltd had during the war it is this one. Probably taken from a quayside crane it shows the Cammell Laird Shipbuilding Yard in autumn 1940. The Outer Basin is in the centre of the photograph and one of the yard's many graving docks on the far left. On the right are two light cruisers, the finished HMS *Dido* and her sister ship HMS *Charybdis*. In the background is the battleship HMS *Prince of Wales*, at this time still under construction. In August 1940 bombs fell on the yard, falling between the battleship and the basin wall and exploding under the ship. This caused buckling of the hull and serious flooding which led to a ten degree list. The ship's pumping system was not yet in use, but local fire fighters and shipyard workers managed to pump the water out. She was later put into dry-dock for repairs that delayed her commissioning until January 1941. In a short but eventful career she took part in the fight against the German battleship *Bismarck*, transported Winston Churchill across the Atlantic to meet the American President and served in the Mediterranean on convoy duty. She was sunk by Japanese shore-based aircraft in December 1941 whilst operating near Singapore.

The modern photograph was taken from St Mary's Tower which is some way behind and to the left of where the wartime original was taken. The tower provides a superb vantage point over not just the shipyard, but also the Liverpool shoreline and Birkenhead Town Centre. For this reason access to it during wartime was probably restricted.

As can be seen from the road sign this photograph was taken in Union Street, close to its junction with New Chester Road. The street was struck twice in the space of a month, first of all on the night of 17/18 September 1940, then later on the night of 13/14 October. This photograph was taken after the September raid and probably shows only the upper floor of number 226 New Chester Road – note the double bed in the centre of the photograph. No-one was killed in the street on either night, but a chilling reminder of the deadly talents the Luftwaffe were never far away. Just on the other side of 226 was 1 Rose Cottages, where Lucy and George Horby, a married couple were killed. In the same house at the time was Joseph Sailer who also fell. The occupants of number 224 New Chester Road, Emily Chadwick and her daughters Rebecca Chadwick and Edith Ferrer were victims as well. They were not at home though, staying instead in nearby Warren Gardens at the time. On the far side of New Chester Road stood a petrol and service station, the pumps for which can just be made out on the far right of the photograph.

This section of New Chester Road is quite different today, with modern business premises occupying both sides of it, including the site of Rose Cottages. The nearest buildings that survived the war and are still standing today are two public houses. The Raglan which stands on the opposite corner of Union Street is still open today, but the Manor Hotel which stood a little further up Union Street has now closed.

Westdale Road in Rock Ferry runs from Albany Road to Southdale Road, not far from Victoria Park. On the night of 24/25 June 1941 the area around the road's junction with Southdale Road was hit by at least one high explosive bomb, causing the damage seen here. In this photograph the building on the far left is in Southdale Road, whereas the others are all in Westdale Road. Four people were killed that night in the immediate vicinity. At number 48 Southdale Road John Clinton (17) and James Bell (35) fell, whilst next door at number 46 Doris Sennett (39) and her daughter Beryl (17) were also victims. These two houses would be just out of shot on the right. A little further down Southdale Road at number 66 Arthur Birch (13) died. Despite the extensive damage to the house on the left the residents survived the raid, suggesting either that they were absent at the time, or were able to get to either a public or private shelter just in time. The presence of the lorry and workers in the foreground, combined with the abundance of rubble still on the road surface suggests that this photograph was probably taken shortly after the raid, perhaps even the morning after it.

The houses in this area were repaired, leaving no indication of the death and suffering the residents of these roads once endured. At the far end of Westdale Road the triangular roof of Well Lane Police Station can just be made out.

Running between Mount Road and Borough Road in Tranmere, Irvine Road was a victim of the raids during early May 1941. The houses shown here are numbers 22 and 24 and are seen from the rear. No-one was killed in either house and although all the windows were shattered and many of the roof tiles dislodged, both appear to be structurally sound. The photographer was standing on the playing fields of the Birkenhead Institute (the perimeter fence for which can be seen in front of the houses). Opened

in 1889, the Grammar School originally stood in Whetstone Lane. Perhaps its most famous former pupil was Wilfred Owen, a soldier and poet who served in the British Army during the First World War (at the time of this raid still known as the Great War). His poetry is widely regarded as some of the finest and most realistic produced during that terrible conflict, often describing its horrors in detail. He was sadly killed just a week before the Armistice whilst leading an attack on an enemy-held village. Irvine Road is named after another local hero, Sandy Irvine. In 1924 he and George Mallory tried to conquer Mount Everest, but died somewhere near the summit of the mountain. Debate still continues as to whether they managed to conquer the mountain and died on the way down, or fell in the attempt. In the climber's honour many of the nearby roads bear the name of a mountain.

Both houses were repaired and remain standing today, this modern comparison was taken from the front of the house as the playing fields are not usually open to the public.

At first glance the damage to the building in this photograph seems slight. It would therefore be difficult to imagine any fatalities occurring here as a result of the raid, which took place on the night of 31 August/1 September 1940. Sadly fate can be cruel to some and kind to others. The same bomb or stick of bombs that brought down a few roofing tiles also killed two people in this vicinity. Just out of shot to the right is the junction of Bedford Drive (seen in the foreground), Bedford Avenue (a continuation of Bedford Drive) and Bebington Road (just about visible on the far right of the photograph). Near here two people were caught in the blast of a bomb. Joan Bywater, an eighteen year old died where she fell. Thomas Hough, who was 26 years old was badly injured and was rushed to the Municipal Hospital in Church Road. Sadly he died there on 1 September. The trees in the background on the right are on the edge of Victoria Park. Someone is standing on the roof of the house, probably checking to see how bad the damage actually was. The white marks painted on the kerb of Bedford Drive were designed to assist drivers during the blackout.

The house was almost certainly repaired quickly and remains standing today. The junction where such tragedy occurred 72 years ago remains largely the same. Today's drivers get their assistance from the likes of the lamps seen on both roads. Although street lighting has existed since the nineteenth century, their use during wartime would have been limited or non-existent due to the blackout regulations.

This tangled mass of rubble is all that remains of 125 Bebington Road which was destroyed during May 1941. The man and woman who are standing on the rubble just to the left of the centre of the photograph are quite probably the owners, since no-one was killed in this part of the road during the war. Although they are no doubt glad to be alive, it must have seemed an almost impossible task to try and pick themselves up and carry on with their lives. Not far from here are the large houses of Egerton Park, which was hit twice during the war. One of the houses struck in the raid on the night of 28/29 November 1940 is pictured below.

This section of Bebington Road is now occupied by small blocks of flats.

On the night of 28/29 November 1940 a high explosive bomb landed at the corner of Green Lawn and Old Chester Road. The house it struck was severely damaged but fortunately no-one was killed. Green Lawn was not so fortunate later in the war as it was hit by high explosive bombs again on the night of 13 March 1941. At number 50 Green Lawn one of them did dreadful damage, killing 10 people. Nine of these seem to have come from the same extended family. Gladys Davies (46) and her 6 children; George (16), Mary (15), Noel (11) Derrick (9), Patricia (5) and James (3) were all killed. Other fatalities at number 50 were Frederick Davies (20), his wife Hilda (23), and Elizabeth Studley (77). Frederick was not Gladys' son but the shared surname suggests that they were related, possibly as Aunt and Nephew. Gladys is not listed in the Commonwealth War Graves Commission's records as a widow so it is quite likely that her husband, William Henry Davies was alive at the time of the raid, but was presumably not at home that night. It is almost impossible for most of us to comprehend how anyone could try to rebuild their life after their entire family had been wiped out in such a sudden and final fashion.

The corner of the two roads is now a quiet empty space that has been grassed over. The site of number 50 (just out of shot on the left) has been left in a similar fashion.

Dacre Hill is the area of Rock Ferry around the junction of Old Chester Road and Rock Lane West. On the night of 31 August/1 September 1940 a high explosive bomb landed in the area, causing the damage seen above. Without a definitive address this photograph proved difficult to locate at first, but a careful study of the building on the far right revealed a sign with the initials "T F". After studying the Gores street directory for the period it was possible to identify this as the premises of Thomas F. Evans, who owned a fish and chip shop at number 455 Old Chester Road. A quick visit to the area confirmed this as the correct address. The bomb seems to have completely demolished 453 and badly damaged 451. The fish and chip shop has had a large hole blasted in its side wall and a staircase can just be made out. The ARP wardens look like they are deep in discussion, but other photographs taken around the same time show that they (along with at least one other worker) were in fact in the process of helping to clear the rubble up. On the same night two bombs landed nearby on the playing fields of Rock Ferry High School, but failed to explode. Fortunately no-one was killed in the vicinity that night.

The modern photograph confirms that this was the location of the wartime photograph. Neither building was rebuilt after the war and the sites of each have been replaced by advertising hoardings. Thomas Evans' chip shop is now a residential property.

Running off Highfield Road, Browning Avenue is one of many roads in Rock Ferry named after a literary figure, in this case the Victorian poet Robert Browning. He was famous for his poem "The Pied Piper" which helped to popularise the story in Britain. On the night of 28/29 November 1940 number 2, which would once have been quite a substantial building, was torn apart by a high explosive bomb, leaving little more than the outer walls standing. The young couple who called it home, Elsie and Joseph Porter were killed in the raid.

Unsurprisingly number 2 proved impractical to rebuild in a similar style, and modern housing now occupies the site. Most of the other roads that branch off Highfield Road are named after other literary figures. Wordsworth and Tennyson Avenues are named after two Victorian Poet Laureates, whereas Ruskin Avenue is named after a Victorian art critic and writer. Kipling Avenue is of course named after the author of *The Jungle Book* and the *Just So* stories. Not to be outdone Elizabethan figures are represented by Shakespeare and Spenser Avenues.

Taken in Railway Road, Rock Ferry this photograph shows the view across the railway line towards the buildings in Highfield Road. The building on the left is the St Anne's Roman Catholic church, completed in 1887. To the right of this stands St Anne's Convent. In the foreground are the remains of a shelter, demolished in the raid on the night of 1/2 May 1941. Remarkably there do not appear to have been any fatalities. In the background on the far right is the Railway pub. On the same night a train was derailed by damage done to the railway line near Highfield Road. Various photographs taken the next day seem to indicate that it was one of several that struck the line as two unexploded bombs can be seen in one of the images.

The convent was demolished in the 1970s to be replaced by a modern housing complex for the elderly. This particular part of Railway Road is now mostly only used as an access point for vehicles doing maintenance on the railway track. Unfortunately the trees in the foreground now block the original view, so this comparison was taken from a higher vantage point and further over by the bridge on Bedford Road. The church and pub remain and provide a good reference point.

Rock Lane East is just off New Chester Road in Rock Ferry. On the night of 4/5 September 1940 high explosive bombs landed in the road, shattering number 75 and killing the owner, Sidney Pentland. Despite the best efforts of the rescue workers who are picking their way across the rubble it is unlikely that there were any survivors here. This section of Rock Lane East (opposite the junction with Chatsworth Road) is close to the entrance to Rock Park, an area of large villas built between 1837 and 1850. The houses were originally owned by businessmen who worked in Liverpool and commuted to work by using the nearby ferry. Number 26 was once the home of Nathaniel Hawthorne, an American author who was serving as the US Consul in Liverpool during the 1850s. When first built the park charged non-residents a fee to enter! The towers just visible in the background of the photograph are probably part of Alpha Drive School. Just before the outbreak of war the nearby ferry closed due to lack of passengers.

The site of number 75 is now occupied by modern housing. The face of Rock Park was changed drastically by the construction of the New Ferry bypass which bisects the park. In the process nine houses were demolished, including Nathaniel Hawthorne's former residence. The majority of the remaining buildings have listed status and have been protected as part of a conservation area since 1979. The author grew up in Chatsworth Road, oblivious until recently of how a man's life had once been abruptly snuffed out less than 50 yards away.

St Peter's church in Rock Ferry was consecrated in 1842 and stands in St Peter's Road. On the night of 4/5 September 1940 the church suffered damage, possibly from bombs dropped by the same plane that destroyed number 75 Rock Lane East (see previous page). The church and nearby vicarage were damaged again on the night of 12/13 March 1941 by parachute mines, rendering both unusable. The wartime photograph was taken after this second raid and shows the view of the church from St Peter's Road. Fortunately no-one was killed in this road on either night.

Although the church celebrated its centenary a year later, it remained closed until 1956 when repair work was finally completed. Part of the problem had been that vandals had stolen the lead pipes from the church organ to sell for scrap value. This is a sad reminder that even in wartime some people would seek to profit out of other people's misfortune. A direct comparison proved impossible due to the growth of the trees in front of the church, so this photograph was taken slightly to the left of the original.

In the foreground of this image are the remains of numbers 21 and 23 Power Road, Rock Ferry. They were demolished by a high explosive bomb on the night of 20/21 October 1941 in one of the last raids on Birkenhead. The road is a part of the Woodward Estate. The lorry on the right is actually parked in Woodward Road as Power Road is out of shot on the left. The houses running from left to right in the background are on Coulthard Road. One person was killed in each house in the foreground. At number 23 Agnes Courtenay who was 32 fell, whilst next door Rita Smith who was just 10 was killed. Agnes was a fire guard, possibly a less conventional term for a fire watcher. Her husband Edward was serving as a Leading Seaman in the Royal Navy at the time of his wife's death. The estate was also hit on the night of 22/23 October 1941 when nearby Woodward Road has hit. The estate is on the far side of New Chester Road from an area of Rock Ferry known as The Dell. This tree-lined road wound past several large houses on its way towards Rock Park. One of these houses was also struck and demolished during the air raids. Also at the far end of The Dell was New Ferry Pier. The ferry service that ran from this location closed in 1922 after it was badly damaged by a ship colliding with it in heavy fog.

Both 21 and 23 were rebuilt after the war in the same style as before, leaving no trace of the damage caused by the raid. The modern photograph was taken from slightly further back to give a better view of both roads. The Dell was developed into a housing estate after the war.

Bootle

LOCATED IMMEDIATELY north of Liverpool, Bootle's name derives from the old Anglo-Saxon word for a house or dwelling. The area has been dominated by some of the region's best known families, including the Moore family and the Stanleys, Earls of Derby. The latter family left their considerable mark on the town through roads such as Stanley Road, and recreational areas such as Derby Park and Stanley Gardens.

Although hard to imagine now, the area was once covered in fields, farms and sand hills, along with the occasional large private house. Like much of the Merseyside area the town leapt forward in size and population with the arrival of the railways. In Bootle's case this came through the construction of the Liverpool, Crosby and Southport Railway in the late 1840s. Around the same time the nearby dock system expanded rapidly, with docks such as Alexandra and Hornby added before the end of the nineteenth century.

The work that these docks provided, combined with the town being within easy commuting distance of Liverpool led to rapid growth, and it quickly became heavily industrialised. Terraced housing sprang up around the town to deal with this large influx of people, leaving little or no trace of the idyllic countryside that it replaced.

By 1868 Bootle was incorporated as a Municipal Borough, with County Borough status following in 1888. In 1903 there was an attempt to incorporate the borough into Liverpool but this was fiercely resisted by the residents who had their own sense of identity and civic pride. The borough's coat of arms is seen above. The symbols largely reflect important local families. The stags come from the Earls of Derby, the crowns from the Bootle family and the fleurs-de-lis from the Linacre family. The motto "Respice Aspice Prospice" is usually translated as reflect on the past, consider the present, provide for the future.

By the outbreak of the war Bootle's population stood at around 74,000, although a great many people were crowded into poor quality housing. A report completed in the mid 1930s found that nearly a fifth of all municipal housing was either overcrowded or unsatisfactory. Although some steps had been undertaken to alleviate this by the outbreak of the war, many houses were still suffering problems with vermin, others were deemed dangerous and many families were on a waiting list for new property.

Bootle's wartime experience was especially difficult, with it acquiring the unwanted distinction of the most heavily bombed borough in the country. Out of 17,000 houses an astonishing total of 2,013 were destroyed and around 14,300 damaged. Compared to even other parts of the region this was especially high and perhaps reflects how compact and industrialised the borough was. In terms of casualties the borough lost 414 people killed and 201 people seriously injured.

Bootle's contribution to the war effort cannot be stressed highly enough, however, as it played an integral part in both the dock system and Battle of the Atlantic. The enormous Gladstone Dock complex was home to numerous anti-submarine warfare vessels such as corvettes and sloops which protected the convoys that sailed to and from the port. The most successful unit of these was the 2nd Escort Group, lead by Captain Frederick J. "Johnny" Walker. In just two years of service its six ships sank some 23 enemy submarines, including one famous patrol in which six were sunk, three of them in just 15 hours.

Captain Walker became something of a celebrity around the borough and was fêted each time his group returned to port. In a town so recently ravaged by the work of the Luftwaffe, with a population so heavily connected to the fate of the convoys, he was a hero. Although he was a hard task master and highly professional, he could also have his more eccentric moments, for example playing "A hunting we will go" over the ships tannoy whilst attacking submarines. Sadly Captain Walker died on 7 July 1944, probably from overwork and exhaustion. He was buried at sea, but within sight of Bootle Docks.

Away from the docks many of the borough's industries were already geared towards the sea and required little conversion to be adapted for war work. The town also boasted a number of anti aircraft batteries including one that was set up on the Municipal Golf Club! Whatever the Luftwaffe threw at Bootle, its people coped admirably, trying to keep going despite the destruction and death.

The building that has been almost sliced in two by a high explosive bomb is St John's School, which stood in Brasenose Road. It was struck on the night of 27 October 1940. In addition to the school, four houses in the road were destroyed and a further nine damaged. Despite this widespread destruction a communal shelter just a short distance away survived intact, a testament to its sound construction. Unfortunately 57 year old Patrick Reilly and his 10 year old daughter Norah were killed at number 73, which would have stood just out of shot on the right of the photograph. They were the only fatalities in the whole borough from that night's raid, despite it lasting more than eight hours, during which a large number of incendiaries were dropped. The tower of St John's church can just be seen on the far left of the photograph. The bomb also severed local water mains and sewers which would have made life difficult for the survivors.

Since the war this area of Bootle has changed dramatically. Both the church and school have long since been replaced by commercial premises.

This photograph shows some of the damage done to houses which once stood in Duncan Street, which was off St John's Road. The exact night this damage was done proved impossible to determine as the photograph was undated, and the ARP records make no mention of the street being hit during the raid. St John's Road was hit no fewer than five times during the war, with the worst damage in terms of casualties occurring on the night of 3/4 May 1941. On this night four people were killed in the road, probably by the same high explosive bomb. At number 110 Hugh Reilly, who was 63 was killed. The tragedy was much greater next door at number 112 however, since the bomb killed 24 year old Mary Roche and her daughters Margaret and Kathleen who were 2 and 6 months respectively. Their father, Hugh worked on the docks as a labourer, and would somehow have had to find a way of going on with his life despite such devastating loss. Most of the streets off St John's Road were named after a Shakespearean character, with others including Hamlet Street and Malcolm Street.

After the war most of the streets in this section of St John's Road were cleared to make way for business premises. Duncan Street stood close to the junction with Bedford Place. Numbers 110 and 112 were on the opposite side of the road, closer to the junction with Ceres Street. Some of the "Shakespearean" streets still remain, in addition to Ceres Street Oberon, Hostpur and Glendower Streets survive.

Viola Street runs between Stanley Road and King's Road and was attacked by raiders on three separate occasions. On the night of 20 December 1940 a parachute mine landed between Viola Street and Bianca Street (see the next page), blasting apart a swathe of houses and killed a total of nineteen people. This photograph shows some of the damage done. The gap in the centre was where numbers 36 and 38 stood. Two people were killed at the latter,

Ethel Adams who was 34, and her 72 year old father Henry Stevenson. The rest of the casualties were killed in the houses out of shot to the left. Between the two streets thirteen houses were completely destroyed and another 33 seriously damaged. The next night the road was visited by another parachute mine, but this failed to explode. No doubt any residents who had not been evacuated due to the previous night's mine would have been moved from the street whilst this was dealt with. This relatively short road was especially unlucky as it was also hit by high explosives on the night of 3/4 May 1941 and more houses were damaged. Fortunately for the residents there was no repeat of the first night's horrific scenes, and no-one was killed on the other two nights. The photograph was probably taken the day after the first raid, at around the same time as the one on the next page.

Most of the houses on this side of the street have been replaced by modern flats. This view shows the rear of the flats as their main entrance is on Bianca Street.

This photograph shows the devastation that the Luftwaffe visited on Bianca Street when it dropped a parachute mine between it and Viola Street (see previous page). The archives list the photograph as showing number 25, and this is presumably the most seriously damaged building to the right of centre. At number 37, 50 year old James Mumford and his 15 year old daughter Betty were killed instantly. Alongside them fell 17 year old Harry Swinton. Initially there was some hope for Jame's 12 year old daughter Margaret who was rescued from the shattered remains of their house and rushed to the General Hospital. Sadly she died there the next day. Next door at number 39, Irene Johnson who was 26, Robert Barwise who was 59, and John Kelly who was 34 were victims. The mine also snuffed out the life of Walter Pendlebury who was 52 and fell at number 43. Walter is listed as a "FAP Member" in the Commonwealth War Graves Commission records. This signified that he worked in a first aid party, raising the possibility that he may have been killed trying to help the others. A quick check of the street directories for the period though shows that this was actually his home. The road was also hit by high explosives on the night of 4 May 1941, when several houses were damaged, but no-one was killed.

From Bianca Street the front of the flats that replaced the area that that mine destroyed can be clearly seen.

Benedict Street runs between Stanley Road and Hawthorne Road. On the night of 20/21 December 1940 a parachute mine exploded in the street, ripping apart the houses numbered between 120 and 136. Five people from two separate households were killed instantly. At number 128 Agnes and Samuel Wilson, a married couple in their late 60s died. Next door at number 130, James and Mary Moran a couple in their late 40s were killed, alongside their 19 year old daughter Hannah. Some way down the street at number 110, the 85 year old Elizabeth Little was critically injured by the same explosion. Although she was taken to the General Hospital, she sadly died three days later. Elizabeth Little was a member of the Women's Voluntary Services, an organisation that was set up in 1938 to assist civilians during the air raids. The service staffed rest centres, assisted in the evacuation of children and provided first aid and refreshments for civilians and rescue services alike. By 1943 the organisation had expanded to over a million volunteers and had taken on many other roles such as the collection of salvage for recycling. It is an astonishing example of the resolve of local people that a woman in her 80s would still "do her bit" to help the war effort. The street was also hit on the night of 15 February 1941 when a shower of incendiaries landed here. Although several passed through the roofs of houses, they were mostly put out by the residents. Those that landed in the street were unable to set anything alight and simply burnt out.

Since the raids modern housing has been constructed on the site, each house set back slightly further than the terraced houses that line the rest of the street.

Ursula Street is located just off Hawthorne Road. On the night of 21 September 1940 a high explosive bomb landed here, demolishing number 16 entirely and badly damaging number 18. Fortunately for the people living in the street the bomb, which was one of 24 that landed that night, caused no fatalities. This night's raid was remarkable for the high density of incendiary bombs that were dropped. Generally these were smaller in size and lighter than a high explosive bomb, but they could still do remarkable amounts of damage by setting fire to buildings. When the two types were used in conjunction they were especially dangerous, since the high explosive bombs often shattered windows across a wide area, making it difficult to control any fire started by incendiary devices. To counter the problem posed by incendiaries the authorities set up a system of firewatchers. These were stationed in prominent buildings, observing the fall of such bombs and attempting to douse them before a serious fire could take hold. The government also issued information leaflets to the general public that contained advice on what to do if one of the smaller incendiary bombs landed on their house. Larger incendiaries such as the 500kg were impossible to deal with in that fashion though and required

the involvement of bomb disposal squads to defuse them.

After the war several houses on this side of Ursula Street were demolished and their place was taken by a set of garages.

This photograph shows the junction of Cambridge Road (left) and Bedford Road. It was most likely taken after the raid on the night of 21 September 1940 as this is the only date which the archive records state that both roads were hit by bombs. The raid caused no deaths in either road, but did some damage to the houses on the corner of the two. Bedford Road was hit on five separate nights during the raids. On the night of 2 May 1941 the Bedford Road Public Elementary school was hit by a cluster of incendiary bombs which burnt out the interior of the building (above right). The classroom below contained several highly flammable wooden desks which the fire has left relatively unscathed. This would suggest that the bomb remained in the roof space and was perhaps put out before it caused a more serious fire.

The houses on this corner of Bedford Road were replaced by garages after the war. The site of Bedford Road School (which stood between Hawthorne Road and Cambridge Road) is now occupied by modern housing.

Running between Hillhead Road and Hawthorne Road is Downing Road. On the night of 31 August 1940 number 92 was struck by a high explosive bomb, which smashed the building apart and killed 37 year old Elsie Smith who lived there. The road was also hit on the night of 3 May 1941, this time by incendiaries. A squad of ARP workers appear to have stopped work for a short while, perhaps conscious of the photographer at work on the far side of the road. This particular image, like so many taken in the Merseyside region was taken by the firm of Stewart Bale. The company were specialists in the fields of architectural, commercial and shipping photography and operated out of Liverpool from around 1911. Many famous companies like Cunard, Meccano and the White Star Line commissioned work from them. They were also invited to record events such as the construction of the Queensway Tunnel and both of Liverpool's cathedrals. This experience and trust made them a natural choice for the assignment of recording the damage being inflicted on the region. They also took photographs for companies seeking to record the damage to their business premises, perhaps to use at some later date in claims for compensation.

Stewart Bale Limited ceased operations in the early 1980s. Number 92 (immediately behind the red car) was rebuilt after the war, leaving no trace of the damage inflicted on it.

The gap in the centre of this photograph is where number 72 Sidney Road once stood. There is some discrepancy as to when this damage occurred. The local archive records state that the house was struck on the night of 31 August 1940 by one of the five high explosive bombs dropped on Bootle that night. The records of the Commonwealth War Graves Comission however record that the three people who were killed in the house all died on the night of 2 September 1940. As there is no record of the borough being raided on that night it is likely that the correct date is 31 August. It is possible that the remains of the three were not found (or not reported) for a few days, which would explain the difference. The victims were John Dew, his wife Frances and their daughter Gwendollne. Damage across the borough was quite widespread that night. In addition to this one, another three houses were completely demolished, 27 badly damaged and 71 slightly damaged. In addition six people were killed and 28 injured. Although this was Bootle's third raid, it was the first time the area suffered casualties. The borough's civil defences are recorded as coping well, co-ordinated through wardens telephoning in reports of damage to the Report and Control Centre. This would then send out fresh rescue squads, ambulances or first aid squads depending on what was needed. The lack of damage on the earlier raids could well have been due to the enemy only dropping incendiary bombs, which would usually be dealt with by alert householders and the firewatchers.

Number 72 was completely rebuilt after the war, and no trace of its tragic past remains. In this modern image it is the house to the right of the lamp post.

This photograph shows the Boys Secondary School which was located in Balliol Road. The building was first hit on the night of 11 October 1940 by a high explosive bomb which penetrated the ground floor of the building. The explosion severely damaged the southeastern-most corner of the building (closest to the camera) and did minor damage to the central tower. The remainder of the building escaped largely untouched. Another bomb landed close by in College View. Between them, the two bombs caused eight injuries. Although the ARP reports stated that there was one fatality as a result of the bomb that landed on the school it was not possible to trace the identity of the person. The school also suffered minor damage in a raid on 7 May 1941 when a bomb landed in the road. In addition to the damage done to the school a further two houses were demolished and eight rendered uninhabitable. The image was almost certainly taken a short time after the October raid as the extensive damage can be clearly seen. Even though labour and building materials were in very short supply during the war, it is unlikely that the authorities would have left the building and area in such a state for so long.

Since the war the school has been demolished, with houses built on the site within the last few years. The building on the extreme left of the photograph is part of the Hugh Baird College. Although a thoroughly modern establishment, its roots go back to the Bootle Technical School. This once stood on the opposite side of Balliol Road to the Boys Secondary School.

Located on the corner of Trinity Road and University Road was the original building of the Bootle Protestant Free church. On the night of 28/29 November 1940 the building was badly damaged by a parachute mine which landed in the area. At number 73 (opposite the church) Diana Blackburn who was aged 39 was killed, along with her 53 year old husband Leonard and their 6 year old daughter Patricia. Also killed at the same house was 52 year old Florence Ellis and her 85 year old mother Hannah. In total the mine demolished five large houses, badly damaged fifteen and slightly damaged another fifty seven. Like most bombs it also shattered the glass in windows across a wide area. Parachute mines were a particularly thorny problem for the authorities due to their deadly blast radius. On the night this damage was done a landmine landed on a railway embankment near the junction of Aintree Road and Hawthorne Road, but failed to explode. Everyone within 250 yards was evacuated to a nearby rest centres and a Royal Navy party was able to make the mine harmless. The locals were fortunate, for had it exploded a similar level of destruction and death to the one seen here could have been expected. It would also have caused major damage to the railway line, perhaps even severing it.

After the war the church was completely rebuilt in a modern style. The houses that originally stood on the left of the photograph were demolished, as were those that faced the church.

This photograph shows all that remains of the Welsh Presbyterian church which once stood on the corner of Stanley Road (in the foreground) and Trinity Road (just out of shot to the right). The building was smashed to bits during the raid on the night of 3/4 May 1941, leaving just the single wall and corner tower seen here. The building on the left of the photograph was a school which was attached to the church. On the right the rear of houses in St Alban's Square can be seen. Two power lines for the tram system can also be seen running along Stanley Road.

The church was rebuilt after the war in a style so similar to the original that even the architectural historian Nikolaus Pevsner considered it to be "remarkably old fashioned gothic", correctly pondering if it had been modelled on an older original. Pevsner was actually German by birth, and before the war he taught a course on art and architecture at university in his native land. He came to Britain in 1933 after the Nazi government enforced a ban on Jewish people in state employment, driving him from his job. In recent years the church closed and the building was converted into offices. The original interior was largely removed and a new floor inserted. The school has since been demolished. Although the new building blocks our view to them, the houses in St Alban's Square are still standing.

Bootle County Hall stood on Pembroke Road, close to its junction with Trinity Road. It was originally built in the 1890s as public hall with a large ballroom. Despite being used as a theatre and then cinema between 1909 and 1923, it had reverted to its original usage by the outbreak of the war. The building was damaged in a raid on the night of 21 December 1940. Although no-one was killed in this building a 74 year old gentleman called John James Rowen was killed in his house at number 14, just across the road from the hall. Most of the people living in the road were fortunate as just two nights earlier a parachute mine had landed here but failed to explode. It was eventually removed by a Royal Navy bomb disposal squad whilst the residents of the nearby houses were evacuated. This probably saved many lives as the majority spent the next few days either staying with friends or in rest centres, thereby avoiding John Rowen's fate. Why he chose to remain in his house, or return after being evacuated is not known. One organisation located inside County Hall during the war were the Food Offices. They held records and thousands of ration books here. Most of these were destroyed by the fires that broke out in the building. Houses in this road were also damaged on the night of 3/4 May 1941. An ARP worker has left their greatcoat and helmet on the wall to the left.

Although only partially damaged, County Hall was never rebuilt and was demolished in 1950. For a time the site formed part of the playground for a nearby girl's school, but it is now taken up with office space and a multi-storey car park.

Just labelled as "Berry Street" in the archive records this photograph might have proven difficult to acquire a modern comparison for, especially since this area of Bootle has changed so much. Fortunately the distinctive outline of the building at the far end of the street made the task much easier. During the war this was known as the Railway Hotel and it stood at number 111 Merton Road. The street suffered a great deal of damage in just two consecutive nights, 21 and 22 December 1940. On the first of these a parachute mine landed close to the junction with Merton Road, doing most of the damage seen in this photograph and killing seven civilians. At number 120 Agnes Kayes who was 33 and her 7 year old son David were felled.

Next door at number 122 Duncan McRae who was 41, Thomas Lund who was 58 and Agnes Ashworth who was 56 were slain. Somewhere in the street 16 year old Reginald Boggis was also killed. Duncan McRae was a member of the ARP service for the Mersey Docks and Harbour Board. On the next night high explosive bombs landed in the road, but fortunately there were no deaths.

This is another part of Bootle that has changed drastically since the war, with the houses swept away to be replaced by commercial premises. One of the few remaining buildings is the pub at the far end of the street. In recent years it was known as the Wharf Inn, but it is now closed.

Located at the corner of Byng Street and Nelson Street, this cotton warehouse was badly damaged during a raid on the night of 21 September 1940. This was an especially frustrating night for the local defences as a great many incendiaries landed amongst warehouses and yards. Many of these contained highly flammable material such as cotton, timber and paper. One timber yard was only saved by a group of boys who climbed a fence that the adults were unable to scale, allowing them to enter the yard and put out the incendiaries. Later in the war it became commonplace to remove such flammable goods from the docks as quickly as possible to large storage areas many miles inland. Some idea of the importance of cotton to the city can be gauged by the size of this warehouse, which in turn can be calculated by how small the gentleman standing on the roof seems.

The modern viewpoint shows that the warehouses were rebuilt after the war. The tall building in the background on the left is called Mast House, but was once part of Bootle Borough Hospital.

The Imperial Cinema stood on the corner of Merton Grove and Stanley Road. Originally built as a Gospel Hall in the 1890s, it was used for various different functions before being converted into a cinema in 1906. At this time it was still known as the Sun Hall, the name only changing to the Imperial in 1923. It was in the forefront of Bootle's cinemas, being the first to show exclusively animated pictures instead of showing them as a support to variety acts. On the night of 21 October 1940 the building was hit by a high explosive bomb and badly damaged. Fourteen year old Stanley Cockbain was badly injured by the bomb, dying the next day in the General Hospital on Linacre Lane. Seventeen year old Elizabeth Mushrow, who was

standing outside the cinema that night was killed outright. To the right were a number of shops, one of which called Costigans was demolished the same night. The buildings on the far right of the photograph are on the far side of the Leeds Liverpool Canal.

The Imperial Cinema closed in 1959. In 1960 the building was purchased by the council for conversion back into a public hall. The public enquiry however found against this, and the building remained closed for many years. It was later occupied by a DIY store, before being demolished in the 1970s. In recent years the bingo hall seen here was built on the site.

This gaping hole is in the canal bridge where Stanley Road crosses over the Leeds & Liverpool Canal. The damage was caused by a high explosive bomb on the night of 21 October 1940. This photograph was probably taken only a short time later since the only visible effort to secure the site and prevent people from getting too close is a single sentry on the left. The tallest building in the photograph was occupied by a branch of the Westminster Bank.

The damage would have been repaired swiftly due to its importance to the road and tram network. Today's view is dominated by the Strand shopping centre and Triad building on the left. The Westminster Bank is now occupied by a betting shop.

The gap in the centre of this photograph is the remains of 323 Stanley Road. The building was occupied by Lennards, a shoe shop. The company also occupied number 321. Although no-one was killed in the shop during the raid, the long length of the road meant that it was hit numerous times during the raids. Another victim was the houses below right, which stood on the western side of

Stanley Road, close to the junction with Merton Road. The force of the explosion was so great that even the tramlines in the foreground have been torn up out of the road surface!

The site of number 323 has since been swallowed up by the Strand Shopping Centre which was opened in the 1960s.

Near the junction of Ash Street and Stanley Road stood a Co-Operative store. The basement of the building had been converted for use as a shelter with the entrance being through a billiard hall next door. On the night of 8 May 1941 a high explosive bomb landed in front of the store, blasting out the front wall and collapsing the upper floors into the basement. Thirty two people were killed almost instantly and many more were badly injured. The shelter was very popular, with many sleeping down there and others bringing musical instruments to entertain the children present. On that night it was packed full of people, some of whom managed to escape via emergency hatches towards the rear of the shelter, whilst others made their way out through tunnels to other buildings. The scene must have been one of unimaginable horror, as this would probably have taken place in almost complete darkness since the raid was still going on. Many of the corpses that were eventually recovered were taken to a temporary mortuary set up in Marsh Lane Baths. The next night that site was also hit, this time by incendiary bombs. This burnt the building to the ground, incinerating the 180 bodies held there. Tragically, many of these had yet to be identified.

A memorial garden to the 32 victims in the Co-Operative basement was built after the war and is located on Ash Street. The site of Marsh Lane Baths is now part of a playing area for a nearby school. A memorial board reminds passers-by of the history of the Marsh Lane site and includes poetry about the incident. The site of the Co-Operative store and billiards hall was cleared and is now occupied by the one-stop-shop for the local council seen in the centre of the photograph.

This photograph shows the burnt-out shell of the Mersey Insulation Company, whose premises stood on the corner of Strand Road and Waverley Street. The site was hit during the night of 3/4 May 1941. Strand Road was an important thoroughfare, linking as it did the docks with the heart of Bootle's shopping centre. Close to the Regent Road end was a massive warehouse for the London, Midland and Scottish Railway Company (below right) which was hit on the night of 21 December 1940 and badly damaged by fire. This photograph was probably taken the next morning as several fire hoses can be seen still working on putting the flames out. Several posters pasted to the nearby wall advertise such exotic locations as Australia and India.

The site of the Mersey Insulation Company is now occupied by modern housing.

building was occupied by a shoe shop. To the right of this were the premises of the Catholic Benefit and Thrift Society of St James. Other nearby buildings were even more unlucky. On 30 August 1940 Irlam Road was struck by incendiary bombs which damaged several houses. The raid on 21 December did extensive damage to several houses and gutted St Mary's church, which stood at the junction of Derby Road and Church Street. The church had stood on the site since 1827 and was surrounded by a graveyard where nearly 20,000 people were buried. Most of the roads in this area were named after places in Wales, more evidence of the influence that Welsh builders (see page 129) had on Bootle.

This part of Irlam Road has changed completely since the war. Flint Street, along with all of the other "Welsh" streets have been swept away and replaced by modern housing. This photograph shows roughly where Flint Street would have once been. The site of St Mary's church was laid out as gardens with a memorial stone placed in the centre. Strangely this refers to the church being destroyed by enemy action in 1941, whereas photographs taken in 1940 show that it was clearly little more than a ruined shell after the December raid.

On the night of 21 December 1940 a stick of high explosive bombs landed on houses that once stood on the corner of Flint Street and Irlam Road. The device sheared off a corner of the nearest building and collapsed the upper floors. No fatalities seem to have occurred here on this night. The nearest

Located at the corner of Vulcan Street and Rimrose Road, the North Atlantic Steam Laundry was damaged during one of the many raids that hit Rimrose Road. Sections of the road were hit on eight separate nights, and whilst it was not possible to track down which raid caused this damage the two most likely (based on damage done to other nearby streets) were 21 December 1940 and 3 May 1941. Although the exterior walls of the building seem largely sound most of its windows have been shattered and the interior of the building seems to have suffered some serious damage. Next door to the laundry were the premises of A. B. Dyke and Co, a firm who imported doors. Laundries such as this

were important in a port, as each ship which docked here used thousands of sheets, towels, napkins and other similar items during its time at sea, all of which would need cleaning before it could put to sea once more. The building was struck again later in the war, probably by incendiary bombs which gutted it completely.

It is no surprise that neither the laundry building or door importers are still standing today. Vulcan Street is now cut off to traffic from Rimrose Road. Most of the area is now occupied by modern commercial premises.

Located on Marsh Lane, near its junction with Rimrose Road this large building was home to the furnishing department of the Cunard Line. This was one of Britain's premier shipping companies, transporting people across the Atlantic Ocean in huge liners such as the *Queen Mary*, *Queen Elizabeth* and the *Mauretania*. These enormous ships, each with room for several thousand people on board, provided passengers and crew with space for eating, sleeping and recreation. All of these would have involved the provision of furniture which would have been made by the company at these premises. The painted sign on the gate seems at first to refer to another local shipping company – the White Star Line. Once two independent firms, these two giants merged in 1934 to form Cunard White Star Limited. The site was another victim of the night of 3/4 May 1941. During the war the company's liners operated primarily as troopships, transporting hundreds of thousands of military personnel around the globe in somewhat less luxury than the peacetime passengers would have enjoyed. *Queen Mary* for example usually carried around 3000 passengers, but often carried five times that

number on her wartime voyages. Fortunately none of the three were sunk during the war.

Although the building is now occupied by a door manufacturing firm, it retains much of the original frontage and layout, with even the gate pillars on the far left remaining. Cunard White Star Limited reverted to using the name Cunard in 1949 and still operates cruise liner services that occasionally visit the region.

Marsh Lane & Strand Road Station was opened in 1850 and was originally part of the Liverpool, Crosby and Southport Railway, but long before the outbreak of war it had become part of the London, Midland and Scottish Railway. On the night of 7/8 May 1941 the station was struck, with fire damage done to both the station buildings and platforms. A nearby coal yard belonging to the railway company was also damaged in the raid. No-one was killed in the area that night. The posters on the wall are for popular brand names such as Dunlop Tyres, Mackeson's Stout and Persil washing powder. Persil was made by Unilever, and Dunlop had a large works in Walton where they made wellington boots. There is also an advertisement for the Hearts of Oak Benefit Society, an insurance company. Nearest to the arched entrance is a propaganda poster that featured a riveter working on a ship. The poster called upon such men to "Speed the Ships" and compared their work with that of a soldier, stating that every rivet they put into place was just as important as a bullet fired by a soldier. One of the posters on the far left seems to be advertising some sort of meeting at Picton Hall in Liverpool. Several workmen are present, and a fire hose is still in the foreground on the left suggesting that this photograph was taken shortly after the raid.

This entrance to the station was closed some time after the war, with the new entrance sited on Washington Parade. Later the station was renamed Bootle New Strand after the shopping centre that was built nearby after the war. The posters have gone, as has Dunlop's factory in Walton, but Unilever still have a major set of works at Port Sunlight.

These are the ruins of Chadburn's Telegraph Company which stood on Cyprus Road, close to its junction with Marsh Lane. As the name suggests the company produced telegraphy equipment for use on board ships. They were an extremely successful firm and their equipment was used on famous liners such as the *Lusitania* and *Mauretania* (both of which belonged to the Cunard Line). Founded in 1870, the company liked to boast that they had fitted their instruments to around 90,000 ships by the 1930s. During the war the company turned their factory over to war work, producing control gear for torpedoes. The premises were badly damaged on the night of 2/3 May 1941. The timber yard of Owens, Peck and Co. which stood to the right of Chadburn's was also set on fire. On the far side of

the road Kennedy's timber yards were set ablaze and damage was done to the nearby Methodist church. As an important part of the war effort Chadburn's workforce were dispersed, although the company's records were destroyed. Fortunately none of the workforce were killed, although two men were killed in the Owens, Peck and Co. yard, Richard Williams and Robert Williams. The former was a 77 year old firewatcher.

Cyprus Road no longer exists, its rough alignment is now taken up by a part of Washington Parade. Where Chadburn's once stood is now a supermarket. The company itself never returned to the site, and now operates from Yorkshire.

This pile of bricks and wood is all that remains of the Welsh Baptist chapel which once stood at the corner of Marsh Lane and Malta Road. The sign below the circular window says "Duw Cariad Yw" which stands for God is Love in the Welsh language. The building was struck during the night of 22 December 1940. Also one house was demolished, and 9 damaged on Marsh Lane that night. Somewhat surprisingly no-one was killed in the immediate vicinity. Many people moved from Wales to Merseyside and once here constructed their own places of worship such as this one. One of the more famous was William Jones, a carpenter born in Anglesey who moved to the area in 1860. He was very successful, making a living from buying up large estates, demolishing the buildings and constructing new housing developments. One of these was the Bootle Hall estate which was in this area and another centred on Monfa Road (known locally as the Klondyke Estate). He also built major housing projects in Everton and Toxteth Park. He was elected Mayor of Bootle in 1886 and by the time he died in 1918 he had built more houses in the borough than any other builder.

Since the war the roads off this section of Marsh Lane have been swept away, leaving no trace of

either the chapel or Malta Road. The original line of the road would have run to the left of the houses, roughly where the gateposts are now. In their place the North Recreation Ground (also known as North Park) has been extended. At the time of writing most of the houses on the Klondyke Estate are scheduled for demolition.

The Salvation Army building on Stanley Road was struck by a high explosive bomb on the night of 4 September 1940, doing severe damage to it. Just out of shot on the right is a branch of the District Bank which was also badly damaged. The newspaper stand next door advertises various brands of cigarettes and a show at the Palladium cinema which was on Seaforth Road in Seaforth.

Now rebuilt in a more modern, but still similar style the Salvation Army still occupies the site. The site of the District Bank is now taken up by an office block.

These men are standing at the corner of Marsh Lane (left) and Litherland Road. The buildings in the centre of photograph once included a sweetshop. This belonged to Mrs Marion Howard and stood at the corner of the two roads. To the left of this stood number 305 where two people were killed. Nathaniel Allt who was 46 and his daughter Josephine who was 21 died, but the war graves records seem to indicate mother Dorothy survived the raid. The Corporation Gas Works (see next page) are just out of shot on the right. A little way to the left down Litherland Road once stood the oldest tree in Bootle, an elm which grew out of the pavement. Local rumour said that when the tree was cut down, the "village" of Bootle would cease to exist. It was eventually felled, although by then Bootle had long since ceased to be a village. On the lamp-post is a sign which is hard to make out but it may possibly have been a temporary bus stop.

The site of the sweetshop along with the buildings between 301 and 305 Marsh Lane were eventually replaced by the modern houses seen in the centre of the photograph. Litherland Road, which once ran all the way between Merton Road and St Andrew's Road is cut in two at this point by the bollards seen on the right.

This photograph shows the view along Marsh Lane from near where it passes over the Leeds Liverpool Canal. The metal framework in the background on the right is part of the gas holders for the Corporation Gas Works. This part of Marsh Lane was struck in several raids. On the night of 3/4 May high explosive bombs struck two of the holders, writing off one completely and damaging four others. One was so badly damaged that over 500 holes had to be patched up before it could be put back into use! On the next night more high explosive bombs landed nearby, cutting off the mains supply and damaging several of the adjoining buildings. The works were also damaged in the final raid of the war on Bootle, which took place on 30 October 1941. Gas was an important source of fuel in wartime Britain, making it essential that sites such as this one were kept in good working order. Its canal-side location is a reflection of the fact that the gas was produced through a process involving coal that was brought down the canal by barge. A measure of the fuel's importance can be gauged by the fact that despite the extensive damage done in the May Blitz and the high demand for workers to repair the battered docks and railways, the gas works were back in working order by 16 May.

The gas holders are still in place, although they are usually only used for storage or metering of natural gas now. This comparison was taken from the opposite side of the road to give a better view of the remaining holders in the distance.

This photograph shows the remains of number 264 Hawthorne Road, which stood at the junction with Park Street. The owners had a very lucky escape, as although much of the property has been badly damaged no-one was killed. Both roads have been cleared of rubble and even the uprooted trees have been tidied up. The fact that there has been time to do this for both a major road such as Hawthorne Road and a relatively minor one like Park Street suggests that this photograph was taken some time after the raid that caused the damage. The five workers present are therefore more likely to be helping with the clear up than searching for missing people. Like many of the Bootle photographs the photographer did not record a date for the image, and as Hawthorne Road was hit nine times during the war it proved impossible to pin down the exact date. On the far side of Park Street (out of shot on the left) stood a Higher Grade School which was attached to the nearby Christ Church on Breeze Hill.

Since the war this corner of Bootle has changed, with both 264 and 262 demolished and replaced with modern housing. The large garden has been retained, with new trees planted to replace those

torn from the earth by the bombing. The secondary school has since closed and the buildings are now occupied by Bootle YMCA. Christ Church is still standing, and a primary school associated with it is located on Cornwall Road. Pupils from the school contributed poems for a time capsule buried in the memorial garden in Ash Street.

Located on Aintree Road, close to its junction with Fernhill Road was the firm of Edward Wilson and Son Ltd. They were a firm of tanners and engineers that had been in business for at least 70 years by the time this photograph was taken. The archive records make no mention of the Road being hit during the raids. This is unusual as they include reports from the Chief ARP Warden which was usually very thorough. The damage seen here was clearly serious enough to warrant a mention, so it is possible that the building was hit during a particularly busy period such as the May Blitz. Nearby Fernhill Road was hit on no less than five separate nights. During one the first of these (19 November 1940) some of the damage was caused by an anti-aircraft shell that had failed to find its target and fallen back to earth. It crashed through a roof at number 59 Fernhill Road leaving a large hole. This kind of damage was not unusual during the raids as the anti-aircraft batteries often fired hundreds of rounds each during any given raid. Although this may seem inefficient given the number of enemy bombers that the batteries damaged or shot down, it helped to raise civilian morale, showing the people that the bombers could not operate without reprisal.

The main buildings of Wilson's engineering firm were rebuilt after the war, although the frontage on Aintree Road with its original sign and date stone were left in place. The building is currently empty and up for sale. Fernhill Road can just be seen at the far right of the photograph, behind the bus stops.

This photograph shows numbers 141-145 Southport Road, which stand near to its junction with Earl Road. The road was bombed four times during the war, although amazingly for such a long road, only one person was killed by the raids – Edna McDowell on the night of 3/4 of May 1941. She lived at number 2 Southport Road and was aged just 19 at the time she died. That night bombs also landed at the junction of Southport Road and Hatfield Road (below), causing the damage that can be seen below. Even the road surface has developed a crack running across it!

The house that the Luftwaffe demolished in 1941 has clearly been rebuilt since the war in a style that matches those around it. All of the houses near the junction with Hatfield Road were also repaired.

This photograph shows numbers 18 and 20 Patrick Avenue which is just off Orrel Road. The buildings were hit by a high explosive bomb on the night of 17 October 1940, causing significant damage to both. In total four houses in the avenue were demolished and many more were damaged. The owners of the house on the left have salvaged some of their larger items of furniture, including a sofa, piano and bed frame. These would usually be placed in storage until the family could find an alternative place to stay. It was risky to leave these in the buildings, especially if they were in an unsafe condition. Despite the extensive damage there were no fatalities here from the bombing. This night's raid was comparatively short, lasting around an hour and a half and damage across the borough was relatively slight. More trouble was caused by unexploded bombs, one of which landed in Park Lane and the other in the rear of houses on Southport Road. A bomb disposal squad was able to defuse the former without further incident, but the latter exploded shortly after it was reported, demolishing three houses and damaging several others. The borough was especially lucky this night as no-one was killed at all in Bootle, suggesting a limited number of raiders. This was not unusual this early in the attacks on the region, but worse was yet to come. Not far from here is Bootle Cemetery.

The houses seem to have been rebuilt after the raids, leaving behind no hint of the damage that the Luftwaffe inflicted on this part of Bootle.

These buildings were located near to the junction of Hawthorne Road and Linacre Lane. The building on the far right appears to be a gent's toilet. To the left of this was Ballard and Parry's fish and chip shop, which considered one of its particular specialities to be tripe. This was a type of offal made from the stomach of a farm animal. Although often considered a delicacy in some countries, in the nineteenth century it came to mean something worthless or offensive in the English language. After the introduction of rationing people would often turn to less choice cuts of meat from the butchers. Next door to this was a newsagent's shop owned by Hugh Williams. The sign above the door advertises a popular form of chocolates, Vikings. The firm claimed that they were the chocolates women prefer as they are "for enchantment". Above the door is an advertisement for Craven A, a brand of cigarettes made in Canada and Jamaica. The slogan above the brand name is unreadable, but they are known to have used the rather erroneous claim that they were the cigarettes that "will not affect your throat", an early attempt to counter claims that smoking was bad for your health. Cigarettes were also rationed during the war but were also very popular and often bought on the black market.

Until relatively recently all of these buildings were still standing. They have been demolished to make way for a new development that can be seen under construction on the left.

The ruins in this photograph are all that remains of the original St Andrew's Church Hall, which stood on Linacre Road, between St Andrew's Road and Kirk Road. On the night of 3/4 May 1941 a terrible tragedy occurred here when a high explosive bomb landed on the building. At the time it was being used as a designated rest centre, a place where people made homeless by the bombing stayed for a short period. Fifty six people were staying there at the time of the raid, most of whom had been bombed out during the previous night. There was also volunteer staff from the WVS present. The bomb demolished the building, killing a total of thirty seven people, including five members of staff. The total would have been higher but for the fact that several of those who had been displaced by the raids left the shelter to spend the night in open fields, reasoning that this would be safer. They expected to return in the early morning, just in time to get a good breakfast, but would have been greeted instead by this smashed ruin. After the disaster instructions were issued that all rest centre staff and homeless people should move to any nearby shelter and remain there until the "all clear" siren was sounded. This was sound advice, but unfortunately it came too late for the victims who died here.

After the war the parish rebuilt the church hall, although it is now set back a little further from the main road. St Andrew's church is out of shot on the right.

The firm of Johnson Brothers has its origins as far back as 1817 when it set up business in Liverpool as silk dyers. By 1920 the firm had merged with two large dry cleaning companies to create the firm of Johnsons the Cleaners. The firm had a set of large buildings along Mildmay Road, which runs from Hornby Boulevard to Stanley Road. One of these was badly damaged on the night of 3/4 May 1941, with the interior of the building completely burnt out. Fortunately no-one was killed.

The central building in the wartime photograph was rebuilt sometime later in a more modern style. Although it is still standing today, it is currently due for demolition, ending more than a century of the company's history on the site. The building on the far left of the wartime image has already been demolished.

The large site dominating most of this photograph was occupied by Scott's Bakery which stood at the junction of Knowsley Road (running left to right in the foreground) and Moore Street (far left). The premises also stretched back onto Gray Street (see next page). The bakery was hit twice in the war, the first time on the night of 21 September 1940 and again on the night of 3/4 May 1941. This wartime photograph was taken sometime after the second raid, which did much greater damage than the first. Scott's were a well known and popular local firm, with many small shops throughout the borough that sold bred and cakes. The loss of the Knowsley Road bakery was a major blow, as Scott's were one of the largest in the borough and delivered food across the entire region. Although rationing controlled the purchase and availability of food, it would be even harder to acquire essentials if such important buildings were lost. One of their smaller shops which stood on Peel Road was damaged on the night of 1 November 1940. A high explosive bomb cratered the road in front of it, shattering the shop's windows. Despite the damage the shop remained open for business.

After the war the company moved their premises to Netherton, where they continued to be a popular employer. Every year the firm would hold open days at the new bakery, inviting regular customers and the families of their employers to tour the site. The Knowsley Road site is now occupied partly by a doctor's surgery and partly by a nursing home.

This photograph shows Gray Street, close to its junction with Knowsley Road. The street was listed in the archives as being hit twice during the war, on 21 September 1940 and 7 May 1941. Strangely the only fatality the street suffered was on neither date. On 3 May 1941 when 38 year old George Sutherland was killed at number 17. The large building on the left is The Queens, a large public house whose main entrance is on Knowsley Road. The bars on the windows were presumably to deter burglars. It is not possible to determine which raid this photograph was taken after, although it was probably done the next day since workers are still attempting to clear the rubble that has cascaded into the road.

It will come as no surprise to find that the premises to the right of The Queens (which was actually part of the Scott's Bakery site) were never rebuilt after the war, although a small extension to the pub was added at some point.

Akenside Street ran from Knowsley Road to Hornby Boulevard. The street was bombed during the night of 21 December 1940, the raiders pelting it with both high explosive and incendiary bombs. An entire section of the street was blasted into rubble and a dozen people were killed. Their ages proved that such weapons have no care for their target, with the oldest victim being 68 and the youngest just 7 months. In addition to the high number of people killed, 40 houses were demolished and another 10 badly damaged. The worst affected area was between numbers 32 and 38 where ten of the fatalities occurred. The area was also hit twice during the May Blitz.

Akenside Road no longer connects with Knowsley Road but its original alignment remains, replaced by the modern Deepdale Avenue. Perhaps unwittingly this name harks back to a problem that the area used to suffer – flooding. When drawing up the Rimrose Brook Scheme the board considered several examples that had caused the scheme to be drawn up. One of these was that in June 1933 when flooding in Akenside Street was so bad that it reached depths of 9 feet 8 inches, and a cyclist who was trapped in the currents actually drowned. Nor

was this an isolated incident. In 1918 the flood waters in the street reached 5 feet 6 inches and in 1927 the area flooded no less than eleven times! It is little wonder then that the scheme was considered so vital to the area. The modern comparison shows the view from the junction of Deepdale Avenue and Bowles Street and it will be no surprise to find that modern housing occupies the site today.

This unusual view is of the rear of houses on Bulwer Street, which is off Knowsley Street. The damage seen here was caused by a parachute mine on the night of 3/4 May 1941, which destroyed twelve houses and badly damaged another 34. In a testament to the terrible power of such a weapon an Anderson Shelter appears to have been ripped up. This can be seen by the large curved sheet of corrugated steel just in front of the first few houses. By some miracle there were no fatalities in the road that night. On the right is an embankment for a branch line of the London, Midland and Scottish Railway. Although it once carried passengers along this route, by the war this section was mostly used for transporting goods to and from Gladstone Dock. What seems like the result of a burst water main to the left of the embankment is in fact the Rimrose Brook. A fence would have separated the back gardens from the brook, but this has been knocked down and only the fence posts remain. Several workers are standing on the embankment itself, either surveying the overall site or working to put the railway line back in use. As it carried important goods to and from the docks it was vital that any damage to the line was repaired as soon as possible.

The line to Gladstone Dock was closed to goods trains in 1971. Since then the embankment has been removed and two new roads were built in its place. This modern comparison was taken from one of these and looks towards Rimrose Road and the docks beyond.

Taken near to the junction of Peel Road and Rimrose Road, this photograph proved difficult to locate precisely due to much of this area undergoing change since the war. Help was provided however by the tower of a church being clearly visible in the background, in this case St James' church, which stands in Chesnut Grove. The church was built in 1845. In the foreground can be seen tram tracks, part of the system that connected Bootle with Liverpool. Although the Bootle Corporation's Trams were originally independent, the two were later unified to make running the system easier. To the left of the centre of the photograph a burnt out car can just be made out. This suggests that the building that would have stood in the centre of the photograph may have

been at least partly damaged by incendiary bombs. Unfortunately the photograph proved impossible to date, as Rimrose Road was hit eight times, and Peel Road three. Even though St James' church was not seriously damaged during the war Chesnut Grove was hit twice, with three people killed there.

As the wartime image proved difficult to locate this modern image is only an approximate comparison. On the far side of Rimrose Road are the grounds of a school. Behind this are several roads named after literary people, in this case Longfellow, Shakespeare and Hemans. The latter had a special connection to the region since she was born in Liverpool and later in life lived in Wavertree.

Running between Peel Road and Marsh Lane, Southey Street was badly hit by high explosive bombs that landed in the area on the night of 3/4 May 1941. The view above is looking towards Marsh Lane and shows two groups of workers busy amongst the rubble and devastation. One of the better known images of the Bootle Blitz (below right) was taken in this street, this time showing the view towards Peel Road. In total some 18 people are thought to have been killed here, mostly in their homes, although a street shelter (seen in the centre of the photograph above) was also hit, killing at least one person who sheltered inside.

The demolished houses were never rebuilt. A set of modern properties were constructed in their place. These are out of shot, behind where the modern photo was taken. They were built across the centre of the street, dividing it in two.

Crosby

LOCATED BETWEEN Bootle and Southport, Crosby has a long and varied history. The name has Viking roots, coming from the Old Norse Krossabyr, meaning "the village with a cross". The village is mentioned in the *Domesday book* and shortly after it was assigned to the Molyneux family, whose descendants later became Earls of Sefton. Through marriage the manor passed to the Blundell family, who made their home in Crosby Hall and are still living there today, 22 generations later. The family were strong supporters of the Catholic faith and many of them were imprisoned or fined for their beliefs.

Like so much of the region, Crosby remained relatively rural until the arrival of the railways. Many merchants and ship owners chose to make their home in the area which rapidly expanded both in extent and population. One of these was Captain Edward Smith, who was in command of the *Titanic* on her fateful maiden voyage. The nearby coastline was also very popular with bathers, especially after the development of a promenade and gardens nearby. An indication of how important the area was becoming can be gauged from the fact that the Liverpool Overhead Railway ran a 2.5 mile electric tram route from their terminus at Seaforth Sands up to the town.

The Municipal Borough of Crosby came into being in 1937 and included Great Crosby, Little Crosby, Blundellsands, Waterloo, Brighton-le-Sands and Thornton. The borough's coat of arms can be seen here below. As it was located right at the mouth of the River Mersey, the region also did its best to prepare for the worst should invasion come. The nearby shoreline was covered in coastal defences such as concrete, pyramid-shaped anti-tank traps and miles of barbed wire that made most of the area out of bounds to the local population.

During the war the area suffered a total of 119 people killed and 331 injured. Eighty four houses were completely demolished, 328 were badly damaged and around 18,500 suffered various degrees of damage, although the majority of the latter would have suffered only minor damage such as broken windows.

This photograph shows the junction of Crosby Road South and Pritchard Avenue. On the night of 3 May 1941 a parachute mine struck the corner of the two roads. The four houses on the right that are still standing (albeit with varying levels of damage) were numbers 1-7 Pritchard Avenue. The large group of men on the left are standing near to the remains of number 75 Crosby Road South, a scene of horrific loss on that night. No less than eight people were killed there by the mine which seems to have utterly demolished the building. The casualties included Albert Silvain, his wife Norah and Albert's parents Mary and Frederick. Also killed were Kenneth and Pamela Haughton, a brother and sister aged just 10 and 12 respectively. The other two who fell were John Bradley and Lena Donaldson. Next door at number 71 things were just as gruesome for the would be rescuers, as they would eventually pull six bodies from the wreckage of the building, all from the same family. Alfred Webster fell alongside his wife Adelaide and their four daughters who ranged in ages from 24 down to twins aged just 14. We can only imagine the painful scenes that would have been witnessed by the men in this image, seeing one shattered corpse after another pulled from the rubble.

Numbers 1-7 were repaired and still stand today. Both 71 and 75 were rebuilt at some point, with the original large Victorian properties replaced with smaller modern properties similar to the ones seen here.

Opened in 1908 by Lord Derby, the Waterloo Library stood on Church Road, close to its junction with Great George Street. The building's construction was funded by the Carnegie Corporation, a charitable organisation founded by a rich Scottish American steel magnate called Andrew Carnegie. It also helped fund part of Wallasey Central Library (see page 25). Flanking the building on either side are lion statues on pedestals. The design was modelled on William Gladstone's personal library at Hawarden. The building was gutted by a fire caused by an incendiary which landed on the building during the raid on the night of the 3/4th May 1941. The loss of such an important public building is especially poignant since there was a fire station in Prince Street, just a stone's throw from here. Just out of shot to the left was Waterloo Town Hall, whereas to the right of the library stood the public museum and then police station. Several fire hoses have been run across the front of the building in an attempt to fight the fires that broke out nearby. The photograph was probably taken some time after the raid as the fire has clearly been put out. There is also a civilian walking down the road on the far right, something that would have been impossible had the area still been dangerous.

The library was never rebuilt after the war and the site is now just a car park. The police station building is still standing, but no longer occupied by the force. The former Waterloo Town Hall is now known as Crosby Town Hall.

York Street is a short road which runs between Queen's Road and Great George's Road. On the night of 30 August 1940 a high explosive bomb landed in the street, shattering windows and damaging several nearby houses. One of the buildings damaged was the Queen's Hotel, a public house seen here in the centre of the photograph. On the same night bombs landed on nearby Wesley Street (below right) demolishing two houses. In all five people were killed in the borough of Crosby that night and a further six were injured. Seven houses were badly damaged and 27 suffered minor damage such as shattered windows.

The scene is now quite different, with modern housing and even a tower block in view. The public house is the only survivor, although it is now called The Waterloo.

Adelaide Terrace is a row of large houses that face onto the seafront in Waterloo. Shortly after midnight on the night of 31 August 1940 a high explosive bomb landed in the gardens in front of number 17, causing the damage seen here. Many of the roads in this part of Waterloo have somewhat unusual names which derive from the same source as the area's name. One of the first buildings in

Waterloo was originally going to be called the Crosby Seabank Hotel, but as construction began on the same day as the battle of Waterloo, the name was later changed to the Waterloo Hotel. This was then adopted by the area as a whole. Nearby is Wellington Street and Picton Road, named after senior British generals at the battle, whereas Blucher Street was named after the general who commanded the Prussian forces at the battle. Close by there is also a Murat Street, presumably named after Joachim Murat. This is a strange choice as he was a French soldier who spent most of his career fighting with Napoleon, rising to the rank of Marshal. Although he spent a brief period as ruler of the Kingdom of Naples, and was therefore technically an ally of Britain in 1814, he actually attempted to fight alongside Napoleon during the Hundred Days, but never fought at Waterloo. This makes it all the more unusual that a local road would be named after him!

Adelaide Terrace was repaired after the war and happily remains standing to this day. The Waterloo Hotel is also still in business, albeit now known as the Royal Hotel. It stands a little further down the seafront on Marine Crescent.

Balliol Grove is one of three short cul-de-sacs that run off Riverslea Road, each of which are named after roads in nearby Bootle. The other two are Trinity Grove and Merton Grove. Around midnight on the night of 3 May 1941 a high explosive bomb smashed into one of the corner houses, demolishing it and doing damage to the properties around it. Somehow no-one was killed in the road that night, despite the extensive damage. In nearby Trinity Grove four people were killed in the raid. Violet and William Connolly were the owners of number 7 and they died there alongside Mabel and Richard Nichols. The Nichols' were Violet's parents and were presumably just staying there for a short period since their normal address was Cecil Road in Seaforth. It is unknown why the photographer chose to concentrate on this scene rather than the one in Trinity Grove. The photograph may have been taken a few days after the raid as there seems to have been time to transport a large number of bricks to the area. With all the activity going on it certainly suggests that the local authority and people could react fast to repair and secure damaged properties. This was no mean feat during the height of the May Blitz as the entire region was under great pressure, with resources and manpower stretched thin and often concentrated on vital industries, communication lines and the docks. The houses seen through the corner gap are on Warrenhouse Road.

Today the scene is like the raid never took place, with the houses repaired or rebuilt.

This photograph shows the Wesleyan Methodist church which stands on Mersey Road in Blundellsands. The building was struck by a high explosive bomb on the night of 13 March 1941, doing serious damage to the entrance porch, spire and tower. The bomb also cut water, gas and electricity supplies to the surrounding area, which would no doubt have made any response to that night's raids even more difficult. This damage is possibly what the worker in the foreground is busy labouring to repair. It certainly would have been given a higher priority than the church since the building seems to be structurally sound despite the damage. It is interesting to see a motorbike in the foreground of the photograph, as this would have been a relative rarity during wartime with petrol rationing in place. For a short time the nearby junction of Mersey Road and Waverley Street was closed to all traffic. The church was somewhat controversial when it was built, as it used bricks recycled from the demolition of Liverpool Road Methodist church in its construction. As the older church was in Great Crosby Village the residents objected to the loss of a Methodist church in the village. In response they purchased the Sunday School on Liverpool Road, eventually enlarging it to accommodate the congregation.

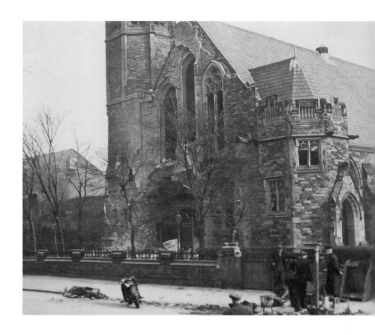

The church re-opened in 1958 after considerable alteration. The spire and tower were both demolished, and another squat tower like that closest to the camera replaced it, giving the frontage a symmetrical look. The stained glass windows (which would almost certainly have been badly damaged in the raid) were also replaced.

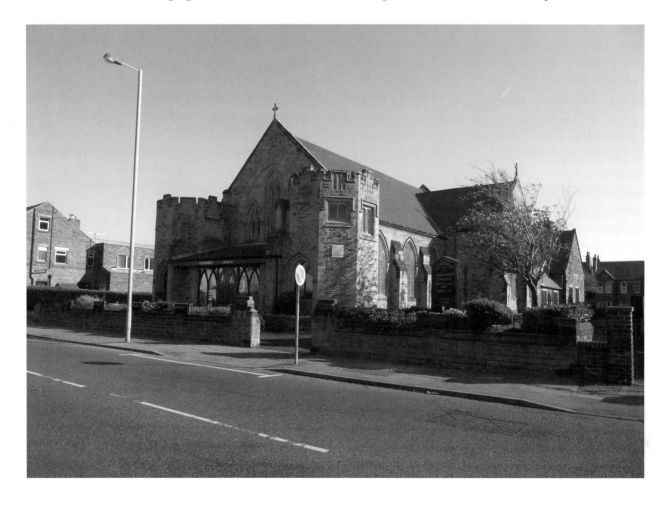

This image shows the junction of Kimberley Drive and Liverpool Road in Great Crosby. The area was pelted with incendiaries on the night of 3 May 1941, and from the look of the damage to the houses in the centre of the photograph a few high explosives probably landed in the area as well. The firm of Armstrongs (below right), which stood on nearby St Luke's Road, was also gutted by fire that night. The firm specialised in furniture removals, and this site was their storage warehouse.

Many bombed out families would have been using the warehouse to store their goods for the duration of the raids. Sadly many of them would have lost these belongings, although someone does seem to have salvaged one or two pieces from the gutted ruin.

The houses on the corner of the two roads were rebuilt after the war, leaving behind no tell tale signs of the damage.

On occasion a photographer will concentrate specifically on the scene of a particular tragedy. Perhaps they were guided there by the rescue workers, or simply because that particular house may have been the one house unfortunate enough to have been struck in the whole road that night. In this case the photographer has captured the shattered remains of number 22 Bonnington Avenue, which is just off Manor Drive. In only the second raid to hit the borough a high explosive bomb tore apart the house around 12:45am, killing three members of the Smith family who lived there. Marjorie, the mother died alongside her teenage children Cynthia and Edmund. The father was presumably either serving in the forces or on duty elsewhere as he was not killed in the raid. The family held the unfortunate distinction of being the borough's first fatalities. This is perhaps why their house was singled out for a photograph, as during the later raids so many houses were scenes of death and destruction that it was impossible to photograph all of them individually. There had been a raid on Crosby the previous night, but the bombs either landed in fields, or in a timber yard on Moss Lane in Hightown. As it was an oil bomb that fell on the yard this might have proven to be especially troublesome, but individual bombs could usually be dealt with quickly and easily.

Like so much of the borough number 22 has been entirely rebuilt in the same style as those that surround it. Even the gate leading into the front garden has gone, leaving no reminder of the horrific scene that would have greeted William Smith on his return.

Caithness Drive runs from Myers Road East to Endbutt Lane. On the night of 22 September 1940 around 12:10am number 36 was struck by a high explosive bomb, blasting it to pieces. Somehow no-one was killed in the raid, although five people were injured. One of those appears to be chatting to a group of people about her experience, obviously not too badly hurt despite having a bandaged leg and head! In the background on the left a group of men are working in the rubble. The next night a high

explosive bomb landed in the grounds of nearby Nazareth House (below), a children's care home run by nuns.

Number 36 was rebuilt later, leaving no trace of the destruction left by the bombers. Nazareth House is still open today, run by an organisation called Nugent Care. This is named after Father James Nugent, a Victorian priest who did a great deal for the region's poorest children.

Running between Liverpool Road and Hatherley Avenue is Mornington Avenue. On the night of 23 September 1940 numbers 1 and 3 were nicked by a high explosive bomb which landed around 8:20pm. The bomb probably landed somewhere in the centre of the road, since both houses were left virtually untouched by the explosion. Even some of the windows in the two have survived intact, a rarity since they would often be smashed by any nearby explosions. In many other parts of Merseyside this

kind of damage would have passed unnoticed, especially on some of the busier nights. As this was still relatively early in the raids and a fairly quiet night the authorities had time to record even minor incidents. The Borough of Crosby was also very meticulous at recording the effects of the raids, compiling a large record book on them in early November 1941. This was done by hand with the help of the Borough Surveyor, and can still be viewed today at the local archives. Across the borough no-one was either killed or injured that night. Three houses were badly damaged, with a further 22 slightly damaged. The worst damage was to the local services, with the bombs blocking several roads and severing nearby gas and water mains. Most of this damage would have been quickly repaired since the local residents relied upon such services.

Given the very slight damage it will come as no surprise to see that both houses are still standing, albeit with slight changes to their outward appearance.

South Road is Waterloo's main shopping thoroughfare, running all the way from the Marine Terrace to Crosby Road North. This photograph shows the devastated remains of the premises of a removal firm called Halls. The company occupied number 41 South Road, mid way between the junctions with Mount Pleasant and Brighton Road. The company's name can just be made out above what had been the main entrance to the building. The building next door on the right was a branch of the Westminster Bank, whilst to its left stood a pet shop owned by John Edwards. Halls was hit by an incendiary bomb, just after midnight on the night of 3/4 May 1941. The bank next door had mixed fortunes, as although it survived the raid which devastated its neighbour, it was hit by an anti-aircraft shell which fell on it around 1:50am on 6 May 1941. The two men in the foreground of the photograph seem to be having a discussion about the previous night's events, whereas inside the shell of Halls a number of men can be seen, presumably working to make the ruin safer. Another photograph that was probably taken at the time shows a young boy approaching the ruins, suggesting that they were both taken before the property could be fenced off for people's protection.

Halls was understandably not rebuilt after the war and its site is now occupied by the modern business premises in the centre of the photograph. The Westminster Bank building is now occupied by a restaurant. The site of the pet shop is now occupied by the Sefton Carers Centre.

Index

Bold page numbers refer to photographs. Numbers in bold italics indicate both text and photograph on the page. Text in italic denotes ships. Parenthesis (curved brackets) are used for clarity.